Lookin' For Love

by
JOHNNY LEE
With Randy Wyles

DIAMOND BOOKS ◇ **Austin, Texas**

Contents

The time was the summer of 1979; the place was the set of the motion picture Urban Cowboy. *I knew I would be just little more than an extra in the movie, singing with the band in the background. I had no idea of what was actually in store for me until one night while performing at Gilley's.*

That night was just like any other, perhaps a little more exciting with the shooting schedule. But on that particular night, in the world's biggest bar stuffed full of cowboy-hat-wearing good ol' boys and tight-jean-clad Texas lovelies, I had just finished a set with the band on stage when a man I had never laid eyes on came up to me and said the words that changed my life forever: "Boy, I'm gonna make a star out of you."

Johnny and Debbie with former President Jimmy Carter, 1987.

Mickey and Johnny with Gerald Ford, 1982.

With former President Gerald Ford.

Showing Betty Ford baby picture of Cherish Lee.

(From left) John Denver, Charley Pride, Floyd Cramer, Wayne Rogers, Betty Ford, Dinah Shore, Gerald Ford, Bob Hope, Mickey Gilley, and Johnny Lee.

With President Ronald Reagan.

Meeting Vice-President George Bush and Barbara Bush.

Beginnings:
Musical Birthright

It seems Johnny Lee was destined for a life of music from the time he was born. His mother, Virginia Callier, named her son after Johnny Lee Wills, the tenor singing brother of country music legend Bob Wills. Virginia first heard her son sing when he was in high school, playing in a band called Johnny Lee and the Roadrunners. It was a group formed by several members of the local Future Farmers of America chapter.

"One day," Mrs. Callier recalls as she sits on her porch swing in San Antonio, "he came up to me and said, 'Mama, the guys need a place to rehearse . . . do you think it would be okay if they came to the house tonight?' I said that I supposed it would be fine. Well, that evening they were all playing their instruments and singing and I wasn't paying a lot of attention. I was in the other room doing something when I heard this one boy sing and it sounded real nice. And I remember thinking, 'Now which one of those boys could that be?' So I walked into the other room and there was Johnny just singing up a storm. I like to have fainted, I was so surprised. I never had any idea that he could, or even wanted to, sing. I just thought he liked to play his guitar. But I was never so proud in my life."

Mrs. Callier would experience another proud moment as a

1

mother in a few years when she would first hear her son singing on the radio.

But Johnny's aunt, Mary Lou Miller, who helped rear him, says he actually started singing long before high school. In fact, Mrs. Miller says Johnny was a talent in the family at the age of two.

"It's just as if it were yesterday," Mrs. Miller says as she thinks back to the late 1940s. "I can still see that chubby little two-year-old boy, in his little terrycloth underwear with his little guitar, standing in his grandpa's house singing 'Chew Tobacco Rag.' He would sing that little song at the top of his voice and stomp his little foot as he'd sing '. . . and don't spit on the floor.' "

But Johnny's musical roots went even further back than that — to a time before he was born. Mrs. Miller says his grand-parents loved hillbilly music, and that kind of music was always going around the house.

"In fact, my dad had a record recording machine in the bed-room, where you could actually make records," she recalls. "At the time, my brother was in the Merchant Marines, and when he and his friends came home they and my sister, Johnny's mother, would record songs on those old 78 RPM records. The boys would play guitars and Virginia would sing."

Lee's uncle, Billy Wilson, also had a tremendous influence on Johnny's life. Billy is a low-keyed working man who thinks for himself. He doesn't do things just because others tell him to. And he tried to share that philosophy with Johnny during the singer's childhood years. Billy knew how important Johnny's singing was to him.

Johnny's mother had married again after Johnny's natural father abandoned his wife and newborn child. But the two step-fathers Johnny grew up with didn't put much stock in Johnny wanting to sing. In fact, they shunned his dreams to become a singer and forbade him from bringing his high school band around to practice at his house.

Billy, however, saw that music was important to young Johnny, so he quietly, and with the love of a father, helped Johnny get his first bass guitar and amplifier. Coming from a family of hard-working people, an expense like that was a sacri-fice. But Billy, like his sister and brother-in-law, wanted to make the sacrifice. "His mother and stepfather came to me and told me that they, at that time, couldn't afford to buy the guitar and amplifier, and asked if I could help. So I did," Mr. Wilson remembers.

Billy reflects, in his quiet way, a pride the whole family shares in the "favorite son" they all love.

"I was always very proud of Johnny," Billy says, "and later in life, while I made it a habit never to butt into his personal business, I would sometimes talk with him and offer advice when he asked. To me he is still just Johnny, my nephew . . . and I will always be proud of him."

1: Trouble Spelled L-E-E

I believe I was a fairly normal kid. I got in trouble some, had fun, got in trouble some more, did a good deed or two, found more trouble, went to church, and would usually stir up a little more trouble before it was over.

Like the time Billy Holder and I told a friend of mine named Stanley that the jock straps we were all buying to wear in gym class really fit around the face as a nose guard. Now, Stanley was a good guy, but he didn't know a lot about sports. So we sneaked some tough-smelling balm in his jock strap before he put it on his face, and told him it protected his nose from infection. Its probably one of the oldest gags guys pull on each other in high school, but Stanley bought the story. When the coach caught him, just before Stanley walked out of the locker room, we bought the farm. Like I say, I was just a normal kid.

I remember Eddie Tyrone and I were in the band when we were in school. The thing of it was, we wanted to play football instead. Now, my folks didn't want me to play football, because they were afraid I would get hurt and it would cost them a fortune if I ended up in the hospital. The fact of the matter was I ended up getting hurt worse while working on my grandfather's dairy. When I was thrown by a damned horse, probably because the mare didn't like my singing, I broke my leg in four places — or should I say that bitch broke my leg in four places. That was worse than I probably would have ever been injured playing ball. So, when Eddie and I decided we were going to play ball, I was already justified in my thinking. I dearly wanted to play, and by God I was going to play. I knew I could from my Little League days. Hell, I was voted most valuable player when I played Little League.

Eddie and I just decided to hell with the band. We figured we weren't going to be band members anymore; we were going to be bad-assed football players. We didn't worry about the formalities at all. We didn't ask anybody if we could play. One day we just skipped band, the last period of the day, told the coach we were going to play, suited up, and hit the field with the rest of the team.

Well, it went just fine and we had a blast. I took to it like a duck to water, as did Eddie. I remember the first time I got my hands on the ball it took several guys to bring me down. Hell, it would have taken the whole town to bring me down, I was so excited to be playing. Of course, as I learned early in my life, all good things must come to an end. I kind of halfway expected it might, but I didn't have a clue it would come crashing down like it did.

The next day, right in the middle of practice, our band director, Mr. Meeks, sent for us. The guy he sent told us Mr. Meeks wanted us back in the band class immediately. Eddie and I walked back to the band house, feeling pretty down in the mouth about not getting to play football, opened the door, and went inside in full uniform. We figured, what the hell, the man told us to get back immediately.

Now, Mr. Meeks was a very low-keyed person who never seemed to get upset — until then. It has always amazed me how people can go from one extreme to the other in such a short period of time, and for what seems to be such a little matter. This was one of those curious times. When he looked up and saw us in our football uniforms, something snapped and he went nuts. He got all white around the mouth, yelled something, and threw his directing baton at us. Boy, we knew he was pissed then. He jumped over about three or four rows

of chairs, a couple of shocked band members and a tuba, and
chased our asses all over that band hall. It looked like something off of "Little Rascals," him stumbling over instruments
and chairs, waving his arms at us, and Eddie and I running
wildeyed around the band hall in bare feet and pads. Since we
were barefooted and a lot younger than him, Meeks never did
catch us. But we did get in some trouble over that.

I've often wondered what he would have done with us had
he caught us. Sometimes I think he was kind of like a dog
chasing a car; if he'd caught us, I don't think he would have
known what to do with us, though I'm sure he had a few ideas
as he tripped, fell, and kicked his way around. When it was all
said and done, my first attempt at football went about as
smoothly as my first attempt at dating.

My Uncle Billy and Aunt Hazel set me up with my first
date. Her name was Lanis Turner, a very nice young lady
they knew from their church. I guess they figured church was
a good place to find suitable young ladies to match me up
with. The only problem was, at the time, Lanis was about a
foot and a half taller than me. But be that as it may, we still,
that is to say, the four of us — Lanis, myself, *and* my aunt and
uncle — went to the movies. We saw *South Pacific* at a walk-
in theater. Talk about feeling out of place. Hell, I didn't know
whether to scratch my watch or wind my ass. I even remember when I went to the bathroom with my uncle, asking him if
I should try to put my arm around her or try to hold her hand
or what. My uncle was a wealth of sage advice. He told me,
"Well, at least put your arm around her . . . you might try to
hold her hand . . . I don't know, but at least put your arm
around her." I was glad to have had some direction when we
got back to the seats, but when it got right down to the nut
cuttin', I was still on my own. As it turned out, during the
course of the musical classic, I managed to put my arm around
her *and* hold her hand. But I remember I wasn't really attracted to her. I guess I might have been too nervous, what
with my aunt and uncle right there. It cramped my style
somewhat, though in my early teens I really didn't have any
style — with girls — just yet.

The next time my uncle and I got up, I think to go get
some popcorn or something, I asked him if I should try and

kiss her goodnight at the door when we took her home. I think I had drawn on his wealth of knowledge enough for one night, because he didn't say much about it. I figured I had done pretty good until then, so when we took her home, and she and I were standing at the door, I decided to try and kiss her. It might have been fine, except she was so tall I had to jump up and kiss her. Well, I ended up banging my head on her chin, and that pretty well ended the mood and the date. It took me until age twenty-one to become attracted to another tall, red-headed girl. I did meet Lanis again later in life and, I must say, she turned out to be a very attractive lady. But at the time, I was too preoccupied with what to do and how to act to worry much about looks.

Runge Park in Arcadia, Texas, was a performing stage for me earlier in my life. I used to hang out there with my cousins Jimmy and Johnny. They were older than me and I always thought they were the coolest sons of bitches in the world. Jimmy had a ducktail and all his friends had cars, including Claude Sumarall, who had a 1958 Chevy. So when Jimmy and I went to our first dance at Runge Park, we thought we were some tough shit as we came pulling up in Claude's car. It seemed to us like the coolest of the cool entrances of all time. We sashayed out of the Chevy and ambled on into the recreation center where the dance was being held, figuring to blow the girls away.

When we got inside the sock hop, the first thing I noticed was that all the girls were on one side of the room, sitting in a row of chairs up against the wall, and all the guys were on the other side, in a row of chairs up against the wall. Not wanting to look too anxious, we cruised over to the guys' side of the room to sort of hang out with our *compadres* like guys do sometimes. Now, I didn't know how to dance, which can be a real problem at a sock hop, but I figured I wasn't doing good just standing there, so I decided to walk across to the other side and ask a girl to dance. I figured on trying to be cool about it, but it was my first time. The more I thought about it, the more nervous I got. I finally decided to make my move before I exhausted what little courage I had built up.

   As I moved out onto the open floor into "no man's land," the room grew into this huge, cavernous vacuum of space. It seemed like it was every bit of a 150-yard walk across that damn building because I thought every son of a bitch and his sister in the place was staring at me. I would have sworn the wall of girls on the other side was moving away from me with every step, but I finally made it across.

   I had this girl all picked out. She probably wasn't the prettiest girl at the dance, but I figured I'd sort of work my way up. I composed myself, made sure my tie was straight, then ambled over and asked her to dance. To my young heart's surprise she simply looked back at me and said, "No."

   "No?"

   "No."

   I was embarrassed to death.

   Well, finally I got to dance with somebody after I built my courage up — again. I was so glad to have a girl to dance with that I didn't even feel the floor when we walked out on it. I got out there, dancing beside my cousin, and thought I was cool. This was around the time when people were just beginning to dance apart. I was acting about as crazy as I could on two feet when suddenly I fell right on my ass. Everybody was looking at me and pointing, and I was so embarrassed that I couldn't even finish the dance. I just walked back to the side with the guys and stayed there the rest of the night.

   Like most people I had several embarrassing moments in my life, and they weren't all during my high school days.

   Once when I was in about the second grade, I remember I was in love with my teacher, Miss Star. Now, the main thing they taught us in elementary school was to never interrupt. But it just so happened that one day when the principal walked in to talk to Miss Star, I had to go to the restroom real bad. I didn't want to interrupt but that bastard kept talking to the love of my life, probably because she was so beautiful. I couldn't wait, and he wouldn't shut up, so I started waving my hands in the air like a flag, trying to get her attention. Finally, she looked over and very sternly said, "Johnny, what do you want?!" That about broke my heart, but I couldn't worry about it then. I had more important things to consider. I told her I had to go to the restroom and I meant right then!

She excused me, but still I had to get to the restroom, which was an outhouse — about 150 yards away. I got about a quarter of the way there and I started going to the bathroom on myself. I was so embarrassed and so afraid, like any little kid would be. I kept on running, but the outhouse just wasn't close enough. I crapped all over myself.

I went on into the outhouse and started crying. I knew I couldn't throw my underwear away because I thought my mother knew exactly how many pair I had and would notice if one came up missing. So I cleaned myself up and tried as best I could to wash out my underwear. It was the worst experience of my life, just terribly humiliating. I did the best I could at cleaning my underwear, but they were still too dirty and too wet to put back on. So, being a dumbass, I crammed them down in the back pocket of my blue jeans, figuring I'd sneak them into the wash before Momma caught me. When you're seven years old and in a tight situation, you'll do just about anything.

My plan probably would have worked out fine if I had been able to go on home, but it was Halloween and we were having a Halloween party. So, I checked to make sure my underwear wasn't sticking out of my pocket, made sure I was all cleaned up and didn't look like I had been crying, then went back to class for the party. I pretty much got away with it except when some buddies of mine kept sniffing and looking around saying something smelled. I didn't have the nerve to tell them what it was.

I had a tendency to be mischievous, which is probably an understatement. I have twin stepsisters, Janice and Janet, who used to believe things I would tell them. They're not so gullible now, probably because of the day I taught them to flip the bird. I did it one day, while my folks were gone. They were little bitty cute girls, and I thought it would be fun to teach them and watch them shoot the bird at my friends. Well, after I showed them they asked me what it meant. I said it meant, "Hello, I love you."

So before long here came my mom and stepdad back home; we lived on a shale road and you could see that old white dust kick up behind the car for miles. When Janet and Janice saw the car coming down the road they got excited and went running out to meet the folks, all four little hands in the air, all four little middle fingers riding high. Of course, it didn't take long for my folks to figure out who had taught them, especially when the twin finks volunteered the information so readily. When I heard my name raised in vain, naturally I hightailed my little butt just as fast as I could — but it wasn't quick enough. Momma caught my little ass, then gave me the ultimate punishment: I had to go get my own switch off a tree. And it had to be big enough for a decent whipping or she would go pull down a damned tree branch from it and beat me to death with it. I always hated picking my own switch. My little butt would just pucker up all the way out there and back.

Of course, I didn't play favorites with my brothers and sisters. Once while we were playing baseball, my brother, Lynn, started complaining that his right side was hurting and that he wanted to quit. I told him if he quit I would whip his ass. See, we only had nine guys to play on each side. Losing one, especially the first baseman, would mean the end of the game, and hell, we were winning! Lynn kept complaining and finally started crying. But I told him we wasn't going to quit, or I'd beat his butt.

He made it through the game and limped on home holding his right side. When he got home, Mom took a look at him, and then rushed him to the hospital. He had to have an emergency appendectomy. I got my butt in trouble again. What made it worse was when I had to sit there and watch him eat ice cream in the hospital and not get any.

My sister Claudia didn't escape my antics either. I remember one day I was riding my bike and had Claudia on the handlebars so she could ride too. All of a sudden my mom called out and said there was a phone call for me. Well, Christ Almighty, that was the first time I had ever gotten a phone call. We hadn't had a phone for very long, so getting a call was a big deal to me. I had no idea who it could have been from, and didn't really give a damn. I wheeled that bicycle around like nobody's business and cut through a ditch, heading straight for the house. When I got in the yard I just jumped off and let it roll like I usually did when I was in a hurry to get off my bike. Except this time, Claudia was still on the handlebars, and I let it go straight into a big tree. Probably that same damned old tree Momma used to get her switches from. Naturally, Claudia and the bike crashed into the tree, splitting her little head wide open. She turned out all right after it was all said and done, but I got my ass whipped nine ways to Sunday. The worst thing was, I never got to my call, and I still don't know who the hell it was.

My little brother Jimmy got me back one time when we were kids by giving me the mumps. I was really sick, with my neck all swollen behind the ears. My mom and stepdad told me I had to stay in bed — true punishment for a kid — and that if I didn't stay in bed the mumps could move down and I may not be able to have children when I grew up. That scared the shit out of me. For all I knew, that meant I couldn't have sex when I grew up! As luck would have it, when my parents went to the store one day, I had to go to the bathroom. No one was around for me to ask if it was safe to walk by myself, so I crawled on my stomach to the restroom. I peed as fast as I could and got back on my belly to crawl back to bed. The whole time, I was wondering if those damn mumps hadn't gone down and ruined my future sex life. Thanks, Jimmy!

I had my share of fun as a child, but all that time I harbored a deep-seated hurt — the hurt of not having a father like my friends did.

My natural father left my mother right after I was born. I never knew why he left. He just sort of disowned us; never wanted anything to do with us. I remember I always wanted to meet him. Lynn and Claudia, from my mom's second marriage, would see their dad when he came around. He and my mom had divorced but he still came around to see the kids, and it made me wish that mine would. When my brother's dad would come and take him fishing they would let me go. But, even though I had fun, I still wished that my dad would come see me and do things with me.

I didn't see my father at any time throughout my growing-up years, except for the back of him once as he walked out of a courtroom, but I was young then and didn't really know who I had seen. He never paid any child support. Never tried to get in touch with me. Never wrote to me. He acted as if I didn't exist.

One time, I remember, I was supposed to go see him. I was still a kid and was very excited. Then, at the last minute it fell through for some reason, and I was pretty devastated. That may be why I'm so envious of people with families, and why I stay so involved with the rearing of my little girl, Cherish. Although she is with my ex-wife, Charlene, I call her almost every day, and see her as often as I can. I remember when Charlene took Cherish and left, my mind immediately went back to when I wasn't able to see my father. It was that same feeling of tremendous hurt and devastation. I want to have a family, to have the closeness. I know someday it will happen.

The first time I actually met my father was right after boot camp when I went into the military. A friend and I went to visit my father and his wife. It's kind of funny, but I remember being nervous about meeting him. I don't recall exactly how the invitation came about, or whether it was given but not really meant, but we went. The strange thing was that he and I never talked while I was there. The opportunity never arose. Actually, after having met him, I don't know if he would have said anything to me if we had been alone. We had nothing in common, and were not in the least bit alike in personality. It was just a weird situation, made even worse when his wife started making eyes at me as soon as we got there.

I blew it off until I felt her rubbing her leg against mine under the dinner table. Maybe I reminded her of him when he was younger or something. I didn't know what her problem was, but I could tell she was being very seductive. Then one night she came into my bedroom while I was in bed and began telling me things she wanted to do with me. I couldn't believe it! My father's wife! That's a pretty strange thing for an eighteen-year-old to have to deal with. I remember getting uptight and finally she left. I never told my father about it.

People used to tell me how much I looked like my father, and I thought we did too. But that was the extent of our similarity. As I mentioned, our personalities were completely different. I'm outgoing and try to be friends with everyone. He, on the other hand, wouldn't say "shit" if his mouth were full of it. But that was the last time I saw him until I became a so-called "celebrity." Then I suddenly saw too much of him. In fact, he tried to sue me for $2 million.

That happened after I did an interview with a magazine reporter one day. During the interview I explained that I had legally changed my name to Johnny Lee. I simply dropped my father's surname and went by my first and middle name, Johnny Lee. I told the reporter I did it because my father never did claim me. Shortly after the story came out, my father had a heart attack. So, some punk lawyer who was trying to make a name for himself helped my father bring suit against me for contributing to his heart attack with that story. Of course, the lawsuit never even got to court.

After that, I never saw my dad again. In fact, I told the people at Gilley's not to even let him in. Once he came to the hospital when I was pretty sick, but I told the family I didn't want him there. I think Uncle Billy handled it for me. According to family members, Uncle Billy met my father out in the hallway and very quietly told him he should leave.

My father had just waited too long to suddenly try to get to know me. I was already an adult and had formed certain opinions about him that were too strong to change. What kind of a person would leave his wife and kid and never look back? To this day, I don't know if he's alive or dead. He's just a stranger.

My mother has married four times, and with the exception of the man she's married to now, Paul, my stepfathers were not much better than my natural father. When I was little, my first stepfather, Bill, would beat my mother. My second stepfather was about the same. All I seemed to hear as a young child was a lot of loud fighting, yelling, and crying. That's probably why I wasted no time leaving when I came of age. Of course, after I split, I soon began to realize how much I loved my mom and my brothers and sisters. We weren't always close, and we fought and argued like most brothers and sisters, but I figured out what they meant to me. Still, I was seeking fame and fortune — or at least some adventure — so I didn't turn back. I was going to join the military.

"They gave me the chair." Johnny, 1946.

Johnny and his mom, with Uncle Jimmy in front, 1946. "I've always loved hats."

Johnny and Lynn, 1949. "We finally became friends after they brought him home!"

Johnny helps brother Lynn (Brownsville 1949).

Lynn, Johnny, and Claudia (Galveston, 1951).

Stepdad Jim Linkey with Johnny, his mom, Claudia, and Lynn (1950).

Lynn, Claudia, and Johnny, 1951.

Grandpa Charlie Wilson

Cousin Pam, Uncle Jimmy, Johnny (with broken leg), brother Lynn, and sister Claudia.

Grandpa's house in Texas City, where Johnny was born.

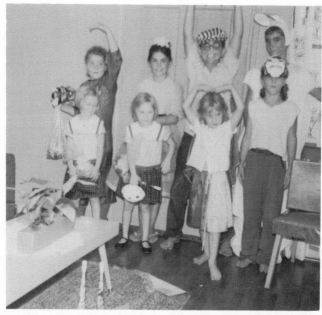

Halloween party at Aunt Mary Lou's, 1960. Johnny has on hat and glasses.

Lynn, Claudia, and Johnny (Texas City, 1951).

Uncle Billy Wilson with Johnny and Tip the dog, 1947.

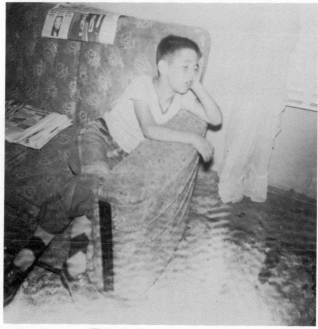

"Doing what I do best," 1955.

"I love riding!" Johnny in front
with Lynn on Uncle Jimmy.

Uncle Jimmy Wilson and daughter
Tammy. Jim was killed in 1978.

Uncle Billy and Uncle Jimmy behind Claudia, Lynn, and Johnny.

2nd grade (1954–55)

4th grade (1956–57)

6th grade (1959–60)

7th grade (1960–61)

10th grade (1963–64)

First pair of boxing gloves.

Dodger Days. Johnny is fifth on front row.

Home on leave, Alta Loma, 1965. Little brother Jimmy and sister Janet.

Johnny's first band: (left to right) Joe, George, Bobby, Johnny, and Claude.
High school hop, 1961.

The Roadrunners at Valentine's dance, Santa Fe High School. Wade Hunt
at far right; Sandra Skillman, far left.

Johnny Lee and the Roadrunners, 1961: (left to right) George Bethume, lead; Bobby Holder, bass; Claude Summeral, rhythm; David Layland, manager; Johnny; Joe Ybarra, drums.

Johnny Lee, 1972.

Faron Young and Johnny on Faron's bus, 1973.

With Johnny Paycheck, 1974.

Johnny Lee International Fan Club

4500 SPENCER HIGHWAY   —   PASADENA, TEXAS 77504

New Member _____

Renewal Member _____

NAME _____

ADDRESS _____

CITY_____ STATE_____ ZIP CODE_____

BIRTHDAY   CLUB RECOMMENDED BY:

MEMBERSHIP DUES: $4.00 U.S. and CANADA
                        $7.00 Overseas

MEMBERSHIP PRIVILEGES: Membership card, 8 x 10 autographed photo of
                        JOHNNY, fan club badge and 4 Newsletters per year
                        (issued in MARCH, JUNE, SEPTEMBER, and
                        DECEMBER).

Member: INTERNATIONAL FAN CLUB ORGANIZATION

Johnny Lee Fan Club card.

Stardom at Gilley's.

Johnny and Ray Charles, 1976.

Johnny with Jay McKinney on New Year's Eve, 1975.

At Gilley's with Floyd Tillman, 1975.

With Mom at Yellow Rose in Corpus Christi, 1975.

2:   Cruising the Gulf of Tonkin

I decided to join the Marines, supposedly the bad asses of the earth. A lot of them still wear those pullover shirts that take liberties with a verse in the Twenty-third Psalm: "I walk through the valley of the shadow of death, and I will fear no evil . . . for I am the meanest son of a bitch in the valley." The Marines are tough and they know it. They're a sharp outfit and always have been, so naturally I wanted to be with the best.

However, when I arrived at the recruiting office the fellow from the Marine Corps was out to lunch. So, I looked across the hall and saw this guy in a sharp-looking sailor's uniform with a bunch of gold on it, and arms covered with stripes. I thought that son of a bitch looked cool — to hell with the valley of the shadow of death and Tripoli and the Halls of Montezuma. This is what I wanted. (There's nothing like the ironclad decision-making mind of a teenager.) Naturally, I waltzed in there and a few simple forms later it was, "*Adios,* buddy, your ass is gone!"

Once I was inside, it was just a little bit different from what I had figured. I left on the first day of November 1963. We were in boot camp on November 22, 1963, when President

Kennedy was shot. I remember everybody was put on alert, and we thought we were about to go to war right then. As it turned out I was sent to Vietnam a year later to serve on the USS *Chicago* — a brand new, first-of-its-kind guided missile cruiser. I'm what they call a plank owner, which means I was on the crew that brought the ship into commission. It was also a flagship because an admiral was onboard and ran things from there.

We were on the sharpest son of a bitch on the high seas. We would sit in the Gulf of Tonkin and launch missile attacks on targets half the size of an airplane, located more than a hundred miles away, and just blow the hell out of those bastards. We had five-inch guns, fifty-caliber machine guns, guided missiles, and ASROCS (anti-submarine missiles).

When I first got on the *Chicago,* I was a "BT" — a boiler tender. It was the worst job in the navy. We always smelled like grease, were always pale from not getting any sun, and we worked our monkey asses off. I remember one of the toughest things we did was climb into dirty bilges covered with oily water and clean out everything underneath the boilers. Then sometimes they would shut the boilers down and we would have to crawl into those bastards and scrub the insides until they were as clean as they could be. We wore gas masks and put Vaseline on us so the smell wouldn't get in our skin and stay on us. It was hot and nasty. And it didn't take me long before I figured out this wasn't the place to be. I put in for a transfer of service to the air force. I wanted to get the hell out of the navy. But my request was turned down with laughter. So, I put in a request to transfer up to the deck force. I got it, and ended up a boatswain's mate. I thought they were just trying to make an artist out of me. All I ever did was paint.

I remember one time I spent the first half of the day scrubbing a bulkhead. I washed it and washed it and washed it, then during the second half of the day I scraped the paint off of it so we could repaint it. It seemed like the navy was nothing but busywork. Sometimes, when we were out at sea and it would rain, we'd have to get out there and swab the decks in the rain — kind of like a freshwater wash down. But at least it was outside where you could breathe and get some sun and see things. I didn't mind that part of the service. And

I have to admit it was interesting being, literally, all over a beautiful ship like that.

We'd work up on the gun mounts or with the helicopters when they'd come in from Vietnam. They would bring in the wounded and they also ferried our mail to us. Occasionally, we would do a little offshore shelling. I never knew what we were shooting at; all I knew is we were doing some shooting, just clearing out some areas. Sometimes we would shell Viet Cong boats that looked like the little fishing boats some of the Vietnamese families lived on. The difference was these boats were armed with fifty-caliber machine guns and would shoot downed American pilots we were trying to rescue. So, when they were spotted, either a chopper would go blow them out of the water, or we'd shoot their asses with those five-inch guns.

Of course, the whole thing was strange to me, that is to say, why we were over there. We had the firepower and the manpower, but it was a political war. If it had been an outright war, we would have just beat them and come back home. But that didn't happen. It was allowed to drag on too long, and I don't know what was proven. Sometimes our guys would go in, secure a position, then just pack up and leave and the Viet Cong would move right back in. A lot of guys lost their lives doing that. Some of the Marines I knew on our ship were sent in and never came out.

At night we would watch the air operations launched from carriers we were protecting. Often we would count the number of jet afterburners taking off. Sometimes not all of them came back.

Every once in a while at night, storms would come up and we would spend most of the night looking for a couple of guys blown overboard from an aircraft carrier. Sometimes we would search and search and never find them. That was always an eerie feeling because there was sort of a brotherhood among the guys. And when they'd call off the search you'd get sort of choked up because it was like these guys were a part of you and then they were gone. When we searched for downed pilots we fought the clock because every minute they were in the water was a minute the VC could get them or sea snakes could bite them — and those sea snakes were extremely poisonous. If one bit you, within minutes you'd be dead. And the

Gulf of Tonkin was full of them in all shapes and sizes, and all as deadly as flying bullets.

I wish we could account for all those boys left behind. I have a strong feeling for the prisoners of war and the missing in action. That's why I do so many golf tournaments and concerts with many other artists to raise money for the MIAs and POWs and their families. A couple of thousand are still unaccounted for. Our government knows they're there and doesn't do much more about it. So, like so many others here at home, I do what can be done to help in any way. But sometimes it feels like we're back in Nam, fighting the unseen enemy.

One thing I can say about the military is I got to see a lot of the Orient while I served. And sometimes we weren't always welcomed in a "friendly" port. I remember we went to Hong Kong and they had to post guards just to keep the locals away from the ship, because they didn't want us there. The guards had orders to fire warning shots to keep people away. We even had frogmen on duty making sure the ship wasn't sabotaged by someone sneaking up alongside. In town, though, they loved the hell out of us and our money. We used to have rickshaw races, drink saki, get drunk, and eat fish heads and rice. Sometimes, to get free beer, we'd go into tailor shops and get fitted for terribly inexpensive silk suits. The whole time they were measuring us, they'd be giving us free beer. Hell, by the time it was over, we'd been fitted for four or five damn suits and be drunk on our asses.

It was just as much fun in the Philippines. The Filipinos were great with music. At some of the bars the band members would have Fender lookalike guitars and basses. They couldn't speak a word of English but they knew those American songs in English by heart, and would sound just like the groups back home. It was great to watch.

The little Filipino girls were great too. They would chase you around over there, and if one of them liked you and any other girls messed with you, they would whip out those butterfly knives and go to town. They just didn't put up with any shit. But we had to be real careful because they were just as apt to stick a knife in their boyfriend as they were a girl who tried to take him away. Those people were really different. That was the first lesson I learned.

The second lesson was to be sure of what you were eating. I remember once I got to drinking their beer and before long I couldn't believe my eyes when I saw a rack of barbecue. Now, I had been out on a ship forever, eating powdered food and powdered milk, so the sight of real food was enough to make me go nuts. Hell, I was a barbecue freak from Texas anyway. I didn't waste any time before I bought that whole tray. After I got through, I found out I'd been eating monkey meat! I don't know how I kept it down. I still love good ol' mesquite-smoked barbecue — but I always take a quick glance around the tray before I grab a piece.

Shore leave or "liberty" was where we always got in the worst trouble, because you didn't dare screw up onboard. Once, we decided to go into town while we were in Honolulu. Enlisted guys weren't allowed to wear civilian clothes on shore leave, so naturally as soon as we got clear of the ship we dumped the sailor suits for some nice "civvies." We had done this before so we knew the routine. In San Diego we had learned to stash our uniforms in the lockers at the bus station. Then all we had to do was go back to the station just before we went back onboard, change clothes, and we were ready. Well, the bus station in San Diego was open twenty-four hours a day, which made it convenient. But nobody mentioned to a few of my buddies and me that the Honolulu bus station closed at night.

Naturally, when it came time to go back to the ship, we were screwed. Here we were, drunk as skunks and no uniforms. When we got a cab and got back to the ship, we all figured out that none of us had money for the cab fare. So, the cabbie agreed to let me go onboard and try to wake somebody up to give us the fare. Well, first I had to explain myself as to why I was now walking across the deck of the ship in civilian clothes. To make matters worse, it was pouring down rain and I was drunk. When I finally made it to my compartment, where I figured on asking some buddies for a few dollars for our cab fare, I just said, "To hell with it," crawled into my bunk, and went to sleep. My buddies were left stranded in that cab on the dock! Needless to say, they rolled my ass out of there sometime during the night ready to whip my butt for leaving them out there. I still don't know how long they stayed out in that cab with the meter running before they were able to get clear of it and back on the ship.

It wasn't always me that got the short end of the stick. We had this guy onboard that was a "lifer," in the military for life. A professional, so to speak. He was a redheaded prick of a boatswain's mate who was an asshole to everybody. We called him Gretta, though I don't remember why. But Gretta would always give trouble to anybody he could, making us do stuff just to be busy. Well, once he gave several of us in our group extra duty, which meant we couldn't go into town. We had just finished a tour in the Gulf of Tonkin and were looking forward to some liberty on shore. Naturally, we were pissed. So, one of my buddies, Gary, went down into the hangar bay where they kept the helicopters and shit into a dustpan. His plan was to put it in Gretta's bunk, because we knew when that son of a bitch came in that night he'd be drunk, and he'd just slide into his bunk without thinking about it. That was another reason we were pissed: Gretta gave us the work, then he went on liberty. Well, I thought Gary's plan was good — but not great. So I made it great. Right after taps, Gary placed that fresh pile of crap under Gretta's bunk sheets, and I pissed on Gretta's pillow. Now it was a great plan.

Sure enough, Gretta staggered in, grabbed the sheets on his bunk, and slid right into that pile of shit — just as he laid his head down on the piss-soaked pillow. I'll never forget the sound he made. We all had to practically eat our pillows to keep from making a sound; I know I damn near suffocated on mine. But if we had so much as laughed, he would have known who was responsible and we probably would have been drummed out of the navy with a dishonorable discharge. We felt like we got that son of a bitch back for being a shithead. After that, he was as nervous as a whore in church around us.

There were some fun times over there, but still, I was just biding my time until my tour of duty and hitch in the military was finished. When I got back to the States and out of the navy, I had to find a job. At first, I considered the San Diego

Police Department. I had wanted to be a cop all my life. I guess most kids do at one time or another, but I seriously considered it for years. What I couldn't imagine was how those poor bastards, in any police department, can afford to live and raise a family on the kind of money they make, especially considering the job they do. I guess they have to be really dedicated to what they do and make it their life's work. Most of the police officers I've met around this country are good people, deserving of respect by the people they protect.

I really did consider it for a while after the service, but I guess the thought of putting on another uniform just didn't appeal that much to me at the time. After I decided against the police department I left California and drove back to Texas. That's when I went to work for my Uncle Jimmy in the building business — and hated it. It was hard, hot work in lousy weather. I didn't like freezing my ass off, and I didn't like hitting my fingers with a hammer, nor did I care a lot for getting itchy applying insulation. But my uncle was going to teach me the business from the ground up. I guess he figured on making me as successful in the home building business as he had been. My first job on the road to success was cleaning up trash around the building sites — a bullshit job, but Uncle Jimmy thought that was the best way to learn.

Jimmy and I were always close. We talked a lot together. He always wanted me to be successful. I remember when I was a kid he would put me underneath on his bicycle and I'd pedal while he steered. We got along great. I always kind of idolized Uncle Jimmy. I loved Uncle Billy, too, but I guess Jimmy was a little closer to my age and seemed more like me. Uncle Billy had already met Aunt Hazel and was married, but Jimmy was single and always seemed to have girls around. He was a cool, flashy dresser and either had a pocket full of money or none at all, but more often than not he was loaded. Jimmy was a wheeler-dealer. I remember he used to show me checks he'd get for thirty, forty, fifty, even a hundred thousand dollars, and I was always impressed. It was a lifestyle I thought was great, and so did he, until he met the love of his life and finally settled down in a big house with his pretty wife and beautiful kids.

One time I skipped school with a guy and we hitchhiked

up to Houston to see this fellow's sister. She had fallen out of a roller coaster and we were going to visit her. On the way back, just before we got out of the Houston city limits, the Houston police got us on the freeway. We were so close I could see the city limits sign, not even a hundred yards away, but they nailed us for hitchhiking on the freeway and took us to jail. On the way downtown, those cops scared us to death. Hell, we were just kids. They told us we were going to have to be good or else there were some big dogs in the jail that would eat our asses up.

Well, Jimmy came and got me out of jail — without any long bullshit lecture. I guess he figured I had learned my lesson. But I had to work off the bail, so I went to work for him, scraping off lumps of concrete on floors before they laid the carpets in the houses he built. That's another bullshit job. I remember I thought he was working me too hard so I just got pissed off one day and started heading off down the alley. He finally drove up and caught me, but I told him I had to stand my ground that time. I wasn't going to scrape any more dadgum concrete. He thought for a minute and then decided he would graduate me up to the next job, which was as a helper on a framing crew. That was a better job, because it was actual carpentry work and you could see your efforts result in a house. It also paid a little better.

After I started working at Gilley's, Jimmy would often come see me. He had a nice townhouse in Houston and a big Lincoln Continental with a moon roof. Sometimes I would be booked for a job somewhere and he would just show up with a limousine and we'd go together in style. He was always the high roller, which is probably where I got that from.

Then one night he backed out of some parking lot in Houston, and a guy came by and clipped his car and didn't stop. Uncle Jimmy went after him. He finally caught up with the guy at a traffic light. Jimmy got out and walked up to the car. Just as he got to the driver's window, the man pulled out a nine-millimeter pistol and unloaded it into Jimmy's face and left him there.

I was a pallbearer at my uncle's funeral. He was one of my closest friends, and I helped carry him to his grave. They had to wrap his face in a towel because that's where the son of a bitch shot him.

The cops caught the guy later and he ended up with a fifteen-year sentence for murdering my uncle. I later found out that he was released on parole after serving only eight years. I guess the price of somebody's life is pretty cheap nowadays. The murderer gets out after eight years and my uncle is dead. I don't know what I'd do if I ever saw the man. I'd probably end up in prison myself.

That sure says a lot about our goddamn judicial system. But then what can you expect from a court system that allows some little punk to burn the American flag? The problem is, if you were to beat a mudhole in his ass for burning the flag, which is exactly what somebody like that deserves, you'd more than likely end up in jail longer than if you had shot him. Still, I know a lot of people who wouldn't be able to just stand there and watch some little son of a bitch burn our flag. I and a bunch of people just like me fought for that flag.

Sometimes I think our judicial system is all screwed up in the way it deals with convicted criminals. I understand that a person is innocent until proven guilty, and that's the way it should be. But the punishment phase of our system should be reevaluated. Maybe we should do things like they do in some countries where, if someone is caught stealing, they cut their damn hands off. It would be pretty difficult to open somebody's locked door or burn the flag without any hands. It would also be pretty damn hard to pull a trigger and leave someone's uncle lying dead in the street.

3: The Lure of the Music

I wanted to be a singer all my life. I really think the music got into me, rather than me getting into music, though I'm not sure where it came from. I lived a lot of my childhood on a dairy that my stepfather's family had in Alta Loma (the town is now called Santa Fe, Texas). I remember I always wanted to work on the dairy, but I had to wait until I was about eight. I thought all my new cousins were cool because they worked on the dairy. And on top of that they made money, real money — sometimes five dollars a week! Of course, we had to get up around two in the morning, depending on how far out we had to ride to herd the cattle so we could start milking at three before going to school. Then we'd come home and milk the cows again in the afternoon from three o'clock until dark, sometimes longer. I don't know why I thought that was cool.

Well, I'd get out there on my horse in the middle of the pasture, where no one could hear me, and pretend I was a singer. Out there I could sing to my heart's content, and if I messed up no one would hear me except my horse. Of course, that might have been why that bitch was so mean. She even threw me off one day and broke my leg and left me out in the pasture. I thought the goddamn coyotes were going to eat me before someone would ever find me.

But my chance to sing with a band came in high school. A group of guys — George Bathone, Claude Sumarall, Bobby Holder, and Joe Ybarra — started a band. They were all in the Future Farmers of America and had heard about a talent contest, but they needed a singer. So, after all that time herding cattle and secretly pretending to be a singer out in the pasture, I had what seemed to be my only chance in life. I went up to Claude and said I wanted to audition to be the singer. Claude thought I was bullshitting him, but he told me I had to have a guitar before I could be in the band. Well, that was just about impossible for me because I only made a few dollars a week.

So, my Uncle Billy bought me this old Fender amplifier and helped me buy an Alamo longneck bass. I don't even know if they make them anymore. Now, I didn't know the first thing about guitars or basses. I thought you just laid your fingers across it, hit the strings, and it made a sound. I didn't know anything about making chords. As it turned out, when I went to audition for this band, everyone had guitars, but no one had a bass guitar. There was one fellow who could play bass, Bobby Holder, so they conned me into letting him play my bass and told me to just sing. Bobby played my bass for the longest time because no one could afford to buy a bass guitar back then.

We went through a lot of names for our band. The Cyclones . . . The Tornadoes. I guess those came up because of the kind of damn weather we have down in Southeast Texas. We ended up with The Roadrunners.

The first booking we ever had was for free. We played at a birthday party for Linda Bentrup, a girl in my class. Her parents threw her a big party at Runge Park in Arcadia, Texas, just outside of Alta Loma. It was a big affair for Linda, one where her family spared no expense to make it a very nice occasion for her and her friends. It was a big deal for us too. My knees were knocking, I was so nervous. We wanted everything to be just right for Linda and for us. We only knew about three songs — all in the chord of C. That was also the first chord set I learned from our bass player. But it worked. The first song I ever sang was "Johnny B. Goode," and I've been singing ever since.

We won all the talent contests we entered, representing the FFA Chapter of Alta Loma High School. In fact, I would imagine that the trophies we won are still in the high school.

The band name eventually changed to Johnny Lee and the Roadrunners. We played for teen hops and victory dances, though there weren't many victory dances. Our high school team at the time was pretty bad, but we had our share of school functions.

Our first big job came from the Nestler's Civic Center in Texas City. A man by the name of Don Burns managed the center. He put an ad in the paper looking for a band for teen hops. By then we had been playing teen hops, bars, and VFW halls and had developed a reputation as a pretty good band. Since the band was called Johnny Lee and the Roadrunners, I was designated to be the band leader and set up the deals. So I asked my Grandpa Wilson to go with me to negotiate with Don Burns, to make sure he didn't take advantage of us. Grandpa was my security blanket. I felt better with him there.

I went in to speak for all five of us in the band. Grandpa sat behind me and I sat across the desk from Mr. Burns. Immediately I was impressed that he had already heard of us. Suddenly he blurted out, "Well, what do you charge? I heard you were good . . . so I'll hire you."

I said, "Well, we'll audition for you."

"You don't need to audition . . . how much do you charge?"

I insisted upon thirty-five dollars for the band per night. He said, "I'm sorry, I can't use you." And my heart fell to the goddamn floor. There I was, in front of my grandfather and negotiating for the band, and I blew my first big business deal. About a second later Burns smiled and said, "We don't pay less than fifty."

I went back and the band thought I was a doggone hero or something for getting fifty dollars a night. That was the most money we'd ever made in our lives. And playing those teen hops at the civic center made us pretty popular around there. Of course, we'd take turns using our homes for places to practice, and out in the country where everyone could hear because it was so quiet, they'd come around and listen to us play. But it was a show in Palacios, Texas, one night that convinced me I had picked the right business.

I was singing a song called "Oh, Donna," and there was a girl on the front row, a pretty little thing, named Donna. The way she looked at me when I sang that song told me that was where I belonged. I ended up talking to Donna and kissed her goodbye. Her friends kept saying they could smell rice burning. It wasn't until afterwards that I found out her last name was Rice. I'll probably never see her again in my life — but I'll never forget the way it made me feel.

I couldn't think of anything better than singing for money and having pretty girls look at me like that. Later that night we all damn near got killed by a train while we were driving back in our 1954 Pontiac loaded with our equipment — but it was worth it.

We finally got enough money among us to buy some studio time and record a couple of songs that I wrote called "My Little Angel" and "The Town of No Return," about Texas City.

Don Burns liked us so well he wound up as our manager. The only thing was, Burns insisted his name go below the titles of the songs on the record, and little did I know that that was where the writer's name went. So, from the very first record that I recorded, I got screwed.

The first recording session had all of us nervous. We laid everything at once, because we didn't know anything about laying in a guitar here or there or anything like that. In fact, when I was young I thought that Connie Francis was such an amazing star because she could sing with herself — even harmonize with herself. I thought she had split vocal chords or something. I didn't know about overdubbing. I figured that in a recording studio you just played everything like you were on stage. But I eventually learned the process, and even figured out a few matching chords by myself on the piano in the studio.

Now, I didn't play the piano, but I listened to the music and used three-finger chords to discover another piece of harmony background for the song. I would mark the keys of the piano — one, one, one for the first verse and two, two, two for the second verse — then I marked the sheet music to match and laid a separate background track for both songs. After we had the finished product, we wanted to sit there and listen to the engineer play it back over and over again.

I remember the first time that I heard "The Town of No Return" on the radio I was waxing my car, a '56 sunliner convertible. I got so excited when I first heard it coming on that I ran around the car and up some stairs to get my friend to come hear it. By the time we got back down to the car, it was over. I had missed it the first time it ever made the air.

Crossroads:
A Man Named Gilley

At about the time Johnny was taking his licks to pay his dues in the business, Mickey Leroy Gilley was coming up the hard way, too, usually in the shadow of his teenaged rock star cousin Jerry Lee Lewis. Both were from Ferriday, Louisiana, a place that many years ago sat on the banks of the Mississippi River before "Big Muddy" made one of its many thousands of course changes. When Lewis soared to stardom in 1957 with "Whole Lotta Shakin'," Gilley was working in the shipping department of an auto parts house. Gilley told UPI reporter Bruce Nichols in a 1979 interview, "That's when I decided to throw my hat in the ring as far as music was concerned."

Gilley had learned to play piano at his mother's church while he was growing up. He sang religious music with Lewis and another famous cousin from Ferriday, Jimmy Swaggart, destined to be a prosperous evangelist. Many people tell of times when the rock singer, the warehouse parts handler, and the would-be preacher would cut loose together in rare honky-tonk appearances. Observing the three men play the piano, whether rock and roll, country, or gospel, one can see a very similar style. The style has roots that tie the three to the sleepy Louisiana farmland where they grew up.

Swaggart's calling took him down a different path. But Gilley, having watched the overnight success of his other cousin, realized he could do the same thing. He thought all he needed was to record a single as his cousin had done, not knowing the other work Lewis had put into his career.

Part of Mickey's decision to become an entertainer came as a result of his move to Houston, when it was apparent to him that there was no work in Ferriday. Gilley began working construction, while playing on the side for five or six dollars a night, until he had saved $150 for a recording session. But "Tell Me Why" and "Oooeee Baby" flopped, and Gilley was right back where he started.

He finally landed at the Nesadale Club in Pasadena, Texas, where he could nurture his style and venture into new areas of his own. The Nesadale gave Gilley a chance to make a name for himself, as well as keep his pool game sharp between sets. His meeting with Johnny Lee would spawn a whole new culture of local music in Southeast Texas, as together they teamed up with Sherwood Cryer, the welder with a knack for making money. The old barn-style building Cryer owned was renovated, as part of an agreement with Gilley, into a nightclub and named Gilley's. Within six months, Mickey and Johnny were the stars of the locally produced country music television show called "Gilley's Place." It was just the beginning of a roller-coaster ride to stardom.

4: Climb to the Top

I started out playing drums and singing with a trio in a little club in Southeast Texas. We'd go to work at eight o'clock at night and I might not get out of there until daylight the next morning. It was open all night, which was against the law. The old boy who owned the place was paying the cops off down there and they would let him know when there was going to be a raid. So we could always close up early and get out of there before a bust.

While I was playing down there I heard about the Nesadale Club and this guy Mickey Gilley, who was supposed to be real hot. Of course, I was pursuing any kind of opportunity I could to advance my career, and the Nesadale looked like a great opportunity if I could only get my foot on the stage. So one night when I was off, I went to the Nesadale. When I got there, someone pointed Gilley out to me. He was shooting pool. Gilley was a good pool player; actually, he hustled pool between sets because he didn't make enough money during the week to really make ends meet. So I went over and slapped him on the back and said, "Mickey! How you doin', buddy? You don't remember me . . . my name's Johnny Lee. We did a Larry Cain television show down in Galveston."

Larry Cain had a big, locally produced dance show much like Dick Clark's "American Bandstand." Gilley looked at me and smiled as if the vision of the memory was slowly coming back and said, "Yeah, I remember."

I said, "I played before you did, and I had to leave before I got a chance to talk to you. But I heard you singing with the band before I left that day. I just happened to be blowing through town today, so I wanted to stop by while you were here and tell you how great I thought you were down in Galveston . . . real dynamite band you had, man."

Well, then we started shootin' the shit about music and before long he asked me if I wanted to sit in for a set. It was exactly how I had planned it. I wanted to get *him* to ask *me* to sit in because everybody would come up and ask him if they could sit in. Of course he'd have to say no, or there would be nothing but a trail of musicians and singers making their way to the stage every night, looking for that big break. But I still played it low-key and said, "Aw sure, why not?" And instead of doing one or two songs, he had me up there for about a half hour.

The next time I was off and could make it to the Nesadale he had me back on stage. Between playing music and shooting pool we became friends. Within a few weeks, Mickey and the people who owned the club decided they liked me, so Gilley asked me if I wanted a job. Naturally, I wasted no time taking it. And it wasn't very long afterwards that I was headed for Houston.

During the course of things I told him that I played a trumpet, which I really did — in high school. So I had to go buy a horn and brush up on my licks for a while so that I could play with the other horn player in the band. It took some work, but I did it.

Well, Gilley and I worked together for about a year. He soon became a good friend, and we could talk about anything, but usually about girls. I can't remember how many nights we would drink beer and discuss the problems we were having. When he became someone I could trust, one day I finally asked him, "Do you remember that night we met and I told you about the TV show we did together in Galveston?"

"Yeah."

"Shit, man, I never saw you before in my life."

He started laughing. "You son of a bitch," he said, "I didn't ever remember seeing you either, but I didn't want to be embarrassed."

I always liked to tell that story on the bandstand and I would end it by saying, "That was in 1969 when Gilley hired me for ninety dollars a week . . . cash. Of course, in 1981, I was nominated for the Most Promising Male Vocalist of the Year by the Country Music Association and Gilley wasted no time in raising me right up to a hundred dollars even."

When I did get that job with Gilley in '69, I was the band leader. Band leader of a first-rate group in the big city of Houston at the tender age of twenty-one. I made sure the guys rehearsed, I picked out the music, and generally took care of things. At that point in my life I knew it was happening just as I thought it should. Things were going great. It was my first position of real responsibility, and Gilley believed in me. I know he did, because he wouldn't have put me in that position and in charge of the money.

He also stuck up for me. That was proven after the night I got sick while on stage. I was throwing up blood, so they sent me home. After a while I called the hospital. They told me to call back if I did it again. When I did they told me to call them if I did it one more time. I couldn't believe what I was hearing from these angels of mercy. Well, before I could call back I passed out from weakness due to loss of blood. Fortunately, the bass player in the band, Larry Land, came by to check on me after they got through playing. He ended up breaking down my door to get to me. He probably saved my life because they found out I had a bleeding ulcer.

To add insult to injury, the owners of the Nesadale decided that they wouldn't pay me while I was laid up in the hospital. Mickey just told them that he and the band were pulling out if they didn't pay me while I was sick. They paid.

That kind of support from Gilley was what made our friendship special. It wasn't long before we were like brothers — except at the pool table. He was ruthless. I did wax his ass a few times, but all in all he was the better shooter.

For a very short time during that period I didn't work for Gilley. I had met a fellow by the name of Tommy Cashwell, who had a band called T.C. and the Good Stuff, a big horn band in Southeast Texas. Horns in a band at that time were very popular. They were like magnets in a bucket of nails, attracting people from everywhere. Well, Tommy asked me to join them as a trumpet player and backup singer because they were regrouping the band and going on the road. I talked with Gilley and found out we weren't going on the road anytime soon, so I quit Gilley to take an opportunity to travel on the road. I never thought I'd quit Gilley, but this was what I had wanted to do all my life: just see the world while playing with a good band, and get paid to do it. Tommy also agreed to let me sing a few songs every night in addition to my backup and trumpet work. I thought that would be great.

Our first job was in Bossier City, Louisiana, just outside of Shreveport. We had to stay in a little cheap dive motel with no phones in the room. Of course, you could hear everything going on in the other rooms since the walls were paper thin.

That didn't matter. We were all pumped up over getting started on the road. That is, until the union guy appeared at our first rehearsal. I had never been in the union. I didn't even know there was a musicians' union. Needless to say, we had to join before we could play in Louisiana, so the union man got our very first paycheck, which left us very broke. We had barely enough to get to our second job in Atlanta. After a few weeks, it was clear to me that the band wasn't going to make much money at all, so I went back to Texas and reunited with Gilley. That still didn't kill my desire to travel and perform; it was just that working with Gilley was a steady paycheck and a lot better time.

But working with Mickey Gilley wasn't just for fun. It was what I perceived to be a chance to be discovered because Gilley was in cahoots with a recording studio. Jones' Recording Studio was the first place I ever really recorded anything. I had laid down a track or two in high school, but this was the real thing. I had access to go in and work on some things. A lot of times I worked with Gilley. I even had an engineer of my own, Bert Frilout, when I worked. Bert was like a wizard in the studio. He had worked with some big names and was the

big cheese around there. I mean, if you did something at
Jones' Recording Studio with Bert Frilout, you were "shittin'
in high cotton," as they say down there. And it was exactly
what I wanted to be doing.

The Nesadale was the typical blue-collar, unpretentious
hot club in Southeast Texas at that time. As you drove up, the
big neon sign over the door would light up the whole parking
lot. Just inside the door, you'd hear the sound of pool balls
breaking on the pool table to the left, and you would want to
duck because of the lower-than-normal ceiling. In reality,
there was plenty of head room but usually little elbow room;
we kept the place packed.

The band was on a stage that was only about a foot and a
half, maybe two feet taller than the dance floor, so you could
see just about everything that was happening in the place.
That came in handy on those few occasions when fights broke
out. Now, to be honest, I didn't see near the fighting at the
Nesadale that I've seen in other dancehalls. The rule was, if
you started or just got involved with a fight, you got your ass
kicked by a big mother of a bouncer, then you were literally
thrown out the door. Everyone knew the rules, and for the
most part, things stayed fairly peaceful. That's not to say it
was always a love fest, and occasionally the fights would spill
over onto the low bandstand, which meant to the bad members drop the life boats and abandon ship. There's a lot to be
said for taller bandstands. For the most part there was no
trouble, because the folks who came there wanted to have a
good time. And once we started growing in reputation at the
Nesadale, we began killing Sherwood Cryer's business at
Shelley's.

Cryer had once been a welder at Shell Oil, saving every
dime he could to buy a business. He never smoked or drank —
he just sold the vices — and probably still has the first penny
he ever earned. He never spent any money for himself. After
he amassed some funds, he bought a little beer joint and ice
house. Sometimes he even fixed some barbecue to sell to the
beer drinkers. It was one of those places on the side of the road
where you could go in after work when you got your paycheck,
put it down and drink, then he'd cash it and give you the difference you had left over after you finished drinking.

Before long he was making enough money to quit welding. He bought a couple of little convenience stores that sold beer and ice, then a liquor store, and finally a little stop on the side of the Spencer Highway called Shelley's. When the bar first opened, it didn't even have any sides — just a small place with a roof overhead and big fans blowing. At the time, most of the customers were Hispanic. They'd come out and drink and dance a little if there was a band playing, and maybe have some barbecue. It was just a small-time operation, but it was making Cryer money. That is, until Gilley and I started playing up the road at a place called the Nesadale.

People drove from all over the Houston area and just kept cruising on by when they got to Shelley's so they could watch us and dance at the Nesadale, which was later called Johnny Lee's. Cryer was relieved when Gilley and I started playing at another club across Houston, but the crowds just followed us there. He was still losing business left and right.

So, in 1971, Cryer asked Gilley to come to work for him. One of Cryer's ways with people is to try and dazzle them — that's how he has made so much money. He told Gilley he would expand the place, fix it up to hold 300 people, give Gilley a percentage of the take, and that he would change the name of the place to Gilley's. After agreeing to the whole deal, Gilley, the band, and I went back across town to Pasadena, and proceeded to build the world's biggest honky-tonk. Cryer may have thought that he did it, and in fact, he may have paid the bills for every expansion — the mechanical bull, the placement of several bars around the 70,000-square-foot saloon that finally grew to hold over 7,500 people, the adjoining indoor rodeo arena that seated 10,000 spectators, and the adjacent recording studio. But Gilley, the band, and I *built* Gilley's.

The movie that started it all for Johnny Lee.

Johnny, Bonnie Raitt, and John Travolta, 1979.

Mickey, Eric Estrada, Charlie McClain, and Johnny.

Johnny, Morgan Fairchild, and Mickey.

On *The John Davidson Show*, 1982.

Johnny and Mickey with Toni Tenille, 1982.

The "Fantasy Island Show," with guest Herve Villechaize, 1983.

Johnny surprises Mickey with Clyde the orangutan, who offers a friendly gesture. Harrah's, 1982.

Johnny and George Lindsey on "Hee Haw."

Astrodome, 1980.

Johnny and Floyd Tillman, 1973.

Making sure Big Ben had the correct time in London, 1983.

Ed Bruce with Johnny, 1983.

Mickey, Johnny, and Jerry Lee Lewis, 1982.

Mickey and Johnny with Robert Duval, 1981.

Johnny and Steve Howe, with Gold Record for "Lookin' For Love," 1980.

Dodger days again. Rick Sutcliffe, Johnny, and Steve Howe, 1982.

5: Hollywood, Texas

It was the hottest part of the hot season in humid Southeast Texas. Technicians were moving big lights around, people wanting to be "extras" were being herded from one place to another like cattle, and the producer was trying to stay on schedule. We were in the middle of the biggest, most exciting thing to happen in Pasadena, Texas, since anyone could remember. Hollywood had set up camp at Gilley's for the summer to produce what would be a blockbuster film that would rocket all of us higher than NASA could imagine. The time was the summer of 1979; the place was the set of the motion picture *Urban Cowboy*. I knew I would be just little more than an extra in the movie, singing with the band in the background. I had no idea of what was actually in store for me until one night while performing at the club.

That night was just like any other, perhaps a little more exciting with the shooting schedule. But on that particular night, in the world's biggest bar stuffed full of cowboy-hat-wearing good ol' boys and tight-jean-clad Texas lovelies, I had just finished a set with the band on stage when a man I had never laid eyes on came up to me and said the words that changed my life forever: "Boy, I'm gonna make a star out of you."

My goal in life was to be a successful recording artist and to travel around the world and sing in places I had never been. The only thing I couldn't figure out was how to get paid to do it. But I knew I would either do it, or die trying.

I remember there was talk of a movie because of a story written in *Time* about a couple that married after they met at Gilley's. It dealt with who they were and what kind of lifestyle they led, pretty much in line with the plot of *Urban Cowboy*. Actually, the magazine article started out to be just about the large honky-tonk just outside of Houston. But the reporter ended up meeting this couple and getting to know them and their friends and family. The marriage went sour, even though in the movie Bud and Sissy get back together at the very end.

I was impressed with the fact that the producer of the motion picture did a great job of capturing not only the type of people who frequented Gilley's — hard-working, blue-collar types who play as hard as they work — but the Southeast Texan in general. The person who still believes in family and God and hard work. Having been raised in that environment, I quickly learned as a young singer just what it meant to be a plant shift worker to come to Gilley's and lay out some hard-earned bucks for a few cold beers with his buddies and a dance with a pretty girl or his wife — or both if he had the balls to. Of course, the other thing I learned early in life is that the world is full of what many call "pie-in-the-sky" people, or as we call them down home, "blue sky and bullshitters." So at first I didn't pay much attention to talk of a movie, because for so long it was just that — talk. And there was a lot of talk back in those days; it was just about as common as rain down in Southeast Texas. But sure enough, one day some people showed up and scouted the place.

My hopes began to build and my mind began to work quickly about what possibilities lay in store. I started thinking that maybe I would get discovered, and maybe something good could come out of all of this. I didn't know if it would be through singing or acting, but I wanted some kind of break because I had been singing for over eight years at Gilley's. I wanted more out of life.

Negotiations started concerning how much the people at Paramount were going to pay to use Gilley's, no simple process when dealing with Sherwood Cryer, the country boy-made-good and owner of the big bar. Shortly thereafter came more talk about who would star in the movie. That's when John Travolta's name began to buzz around the club, and then the area, and finally the whole town. The radio and television news began to do stories and speculate, and it seemed like the snowball had started rolling. They were also looking for someone to play his wife in the movie. I understand Sissy Spacek, who had become a household name by her stellar performance as Stephen King's fire-throwing witch in *Carrie,* turned down the role before Debra Winger took it.

It was becoming more apparent that the movie was real as the whole town became excited. Soon the big trucks were rolling in and lights, scaffolding, camera gear, and technicians began crawling the place like fireants building a five-foot mound. People would show up every day just to get a chance to be an extra in the movie, and many of them did because the movie company needed a lot of people for the scenes inside the club. I don't even think most of them knew they were going to get money when they showed up; they were just happy to be in the picture. It was all very interesting to watch the movie being made and the people that buzzed around.

Then one night a fellow came strolling into the crowded club. He spent most of the night around the mechanical bull that became a centerpiece for the movie, watching what went on as people rode the bull. He'd drink a little beer and talk with people, but no one really knew who he was, and for that matter probably didn't care. He wore a dark, heavy beard and had dark hair under the cowboy hat he wore. With the exception of a few brief conversations with some of the club's patrons, he said very little. I would never have recognized him, until someone finally walked over to me, with a tilted head his way, and said, "You know who that is?"

I said, "No, who?"

"It's John Travolta."

I remember I looked back and kind of squinted my eyes as I peered through the smoky haze of the club, past the cowboy hats and feathers, until I got a clear look at him. I still didn't believe it, because of the beard. The last I had seen of Travolta was in *Grease* with Olivia Newton-John — and that didn't look like Travolta. Then I got a clear look at him right in the face. It sure as hell was. I thought to myself, those folks don't even know who they're talking to right now. He looked just like he did at the beginning of the movie, before he had to shave his beard to go to work at the plant with his uncle.

After that night Sherwood Cryer or Mickey Gilley would start telling everyone that "Travolta might be back tonight." Everybody would watch the door and get all excited to try and get a glimpse of him.

The first time I actually met Travolta was at the club, though without the crowd around. It was during the day, when most of the shooting of the movie went on. I always thought that I had a big beard until I met him in his full beard. I remember I was in awe of him, after he had been so successful in *Saturday Night Fever*. And just as I had observed a few nights earlier when he was in the crowd at the club, he was kind of a shy guy, but very nice. After that he came out to the club several times to watch people, stand around the bull and watch the riders, and just absorb the atmosphere of the largest honky-tonk in the world.

One afternoon I was standing in the club at the end of the bar, watching things being set up, when I saw Debra Winger walk in looking like a little angel. I was very impressed with her. She was a real down-to-earth girl, and very cute. She was real friendly, and it wasn't long before we became friends. I gave her a Lone Star armadillo pin for her hat that she wore in the movie. I even taught her how to say "bull" the way we do in Texas. She and Travolta both had an accent that wouldn't exactly let them say it just the way we did. I thought that was pretty funny at the time, but I soon realized they were working to make their characters more believable. Of course, learning to pronounce "bull" also helped her say "Bud" the right way, too, with that same Texas drawl. That was pretty important, since her husband's name in the movie was Bud.

Before long there was a script written for the movie, and everyone who was to appear in the movie got a copy. I've still got mine. I'll treasure it forever because it was given to me when the decision was made that I would actually be in the movie. Until then I just thought I was going to be on the bandstand backing up Mickey Gilley. But a fellow by the name of Irving Azoff changed all that. Azoff managed groups like The Eagles and Fleetwood Mac, though I didn't know it at the time. He was the one who stopped me one night as I was heading toward the bar for a beer. I had been singing a set and was taking a break when he asked me, "You wanna be in that movie *Urban Cowboy?*"

"I damn sure do," I told him.

"OK," he said, "I'm gonna make a star out of you, boy."

My first thought was "Yeah, OK, that'll be great . . . I'd like to be a star," and I didn't think much more about it or the short little Jewish guy with the promise of fame. Instead I just went on to the bar and got my beer. Finally, someone told me who Irving Azoff was, gave me a quick rundown of his musical management credits, and mentioned that he could do what he said he would do with little problem. That's when I knew Azoff wasn't lying, and I began to get excited.

Sure enough we started looking for songs for me to sing in the movie. Azoff had been listening to me perform "Cherokee Fiddle" when we met, and he immediately decided that would be one, but he said I would have to record a few more for the movie soundtrack. Paramount was already a step ahead. The movie company had been receiving demo tapes from people all over the country with songs they wanted to sell for the movie. One day the music coordinator of the movie, Becky Shargo, took a big cardboard box full of songs to a hotel room near the Galleria in Houston and told me to come over and pick out a few that I liked.

We had gone through almost twenty songs, some pretty good and others fairly marginal, before I just happened to reach way down in the bottom of the box and pulled up this song entitled "Lookin' For Love In All The Wrong Places." We cued up the tape, and before the second verse had played I decided I really liked the song. In fact, it was great. I related to it so well that I was surprised I hadn't written it myself. As it turned out, the song was written by two second-grade teachers in Gulfport, Mississippi, named Patti Ryan and Wanda Mallette, with help from Bob Morrison at Colombine Music. The duo has since written a few other country songs including "It Ain't Easy Being Easy."

I told Becky that I really liked "Lookin' For Love" and she said she thought it would play well in the movie. Little did we know that it would be the hit song of the movie. I remember when Gilley first heard me sing it he said, "Johnny, you got a hit on your hands, son." I also picked out a song called "Rode Hard and Put Up Wet," which was in the movie, but it wasn't released until the *Urban Cowboy 2* album.

In the meantime, things were well under way back at Gilley's every day, to the point that off-duty Pasadena police officers were being hired as security personnel. The place was like a beehive. And it got real busy for people like Gilley and me, because we had to be in scenes. In my case I was in a number of scenes playing on the bandstand in the background, just as I had been told I would do early on. Then, with the decision that I sing a few of the numbers in the movie, close-ups of me singing and shots of the band and me playing were needed.

We always had to get to the club early every morning, sometimes before daylight. And they wanted virtually everybody there, because if one scene was being shot and something went wrong they wanted to be able to go on to another scene while the first one was being reworked or repaired. So it was, in some ways, like the army — a lot of hurry up and wait. I might get there at seven in the morning and it would be five o'clock in the afternoon before I would shoot.

The movie company used some of the employees of Gilley's in making the film, which was rather exciting for everyone, but we still had to be back at the club that night to work. I didn't realize how tough the schedule was until looking back years later. I'd stand around most of the day shooting, or waiting to be shot in a scene, then I'd be back that night to perform. I used to get tired, but I never really realized how tough it was. I was just too excited about being a part of the whole thing. The long hours and the scores of takes never made a difference to me, really.

It was interesting to see how involved it was just to get a few seconds of film. During the scene where Debra and John met at the club, the band was in the background playing, so we had to lipsynch to a tape of the song that was going to be laid down under the scene. It took what seemed like forever to shoot, because of the different angles the producer wanted. And if anything went wrong — someone didn't dance into or out of the frame in the background at just the right moment, or the director just didn't like the way a particular take "felt" — we would stage it again. It wasn't the hardest work I've ever done in my life, by any stretch of the imagination, but it was work. I have a whole different outlook, not to mention respect, for those who choose acting and filmmaking as a career. It can be as grueling as my business. But I guess that's true about anything you're dedicated to doing.

Still, it was mentally and physically taxing to shoot the various scenes in the club. Part of the problem was the heat. They had to shoot with the air conditioning system off because it made too much noise in the background. And it was terribly hot. Keep in mind that this was at the height of a humid Texas summer. It always seemed funny to me that someone from the staff of Paramount would spend time putting a little make-up on us before shooting, and by the time they got around to filming whatever scene we might be in, we were already so wet with sweat that the make-up was gone. But that added authenticity I guess, since, in reality, Cryer kept the club a little warm. People drank more cold beer when they were sweating.

The movie company was always trying to keep production going because they knew that bad weather or technical problems might crop up with the same short notice. In addition, they had to be through shooting at Gilley's by around seven o'clock on Friday so it wouldn't interfere with the club's weekend business, which, by then, was better than it had ever been. People were coming from everywhere once they heard about the movie being shot at Gilley's. They just wanted to see the club and be a part of the infamous shooting period, so they could watch the movie when it came out and say to friends, "I was there when they shot the movie." It was unreal. Even during the day it was like a Saturday night crowd. People would show up out there trying to see Travolta or trying to get an extra part in the movie. The Spencer Highway, out where Gilley's is, was always lined with cars. Hell, Cryer, never one to miss a money-making scheme, would charge people a few bucks to go in and see the place during the day, when nothing was going on as far as production of the film was concerned. I know he made a small fortune just off of that, and you can bet it didn't go to any charity but the "Line Sherwood's Pocket" fund.

Of course, everything was filmed right around Gilley's, except for places like Cowboy's on Westheimer in Houston, where the character Madeline takes Bud and his family after watching Sissy erotically ride the bull at Gilley's, or at the penthouse where Madeline was supposed to live. Then there was the one outside scene with Debra walking into a trailer behind Gilley's that was obviously shot somewhere else in the country, since you can see mountains in the background. Now keep in mind that the Texas coast is so flat, they have to put up signs to tell the water which way to run. Anyone who's ever been to Houston will tell you there just ain't any mountains down there anywhere — period.

Despite the hard work, it goes without even a second thought needed that the movie *Urban Cowboy* was a great opportunity for me. It was like I had been loaded into a giant slingshot and hurled to the stars. My world became caught up in a whirlwind. Things were happening faster than I could keep up with, which caused one incident that gave me a taste of what some people will do if given the chance.

Anyone who ever saw me at Gilley's or has seen my show knows that I will stay afterward and sign autographs until the cows come home. I enjoy the time spent with fans because they're fun to talk with. Besides, they're the ones who have provided whatever success I've had. But as some fans will tell you, especially in my younger days, I drank a few beers and sometimes would have a little too much to drink by the end of the evening. I think that happens to everyone; unfortunately, it happened one time too often for me.

One night at Gilley's, while I was drunk and signing autographs, a girl brought a picture of me for my signature, like so many thousands had done before. She told me she wanted me to sign the picture for her son. She wanted it to read that it was from his father, as if the boy's dad had arranged for me to sign the picture. For some reason it touched me that she wanted to give her little boy a picture of me and pretend that his father had gotten the autograph. I figured she was trying to build up the father's image in his son's eyes, and I thought that was great. Not ever knowing my own father, I've always been envious of children with dads, so I was glad to help. She said, "Johnny, will you sign it 'To Travis, from your Dad'?" As I said, I was drunk and perhaps a little dumb — in fact, a lot dumb, to the tune of about $14,000.

It turned out she was dating some Houston lawyer with a great idea to make some money. Not long after that, I was served with a paternity suit. She claimed I had fathered her child, and she was going to use my autographed picture as a signed admission that young Travis was my son by her. I had to get a lawyer, almost miss a concert in New York, and settle outside a Houston courtroom for $14,000. I figure that autograph cost me about $3,000 per word. I suddenly knew what fame and a movie could do.

But, had it not been for the movie, I'd probably still be knuckling down, searching for that hit song like so many other country artists. *Urban Cowboy* was responsible for three hits: "Lookin' For Love," "Cherokee Fiddle," and "Rode Hard and Put Up Wet," all great songs and great money-makers. The problem is, hard as it may be to imagine, I never saw a dime from those songs.

There's no doubt that working at Gilley's was good to me, but being just a country boy with no real experience in the ways of the world, it took a while before I began realizing that things weren't right as far as my money was concerned.

I never saw the contract I had with Cryer; I just trusted
him. He was a country boy himself, a former plant shift
worker who had turned a profit in a few small business ven-
tures, then bought a club and made a fortune. Despite all the
money and fame, he still came around in overalls, and the
stiffest drink he might have at the bar was orange juice. So I
didn't ever think I needed to look at the fine print of the contract I had with him, even though he tried to tell me it was
some kind of ninety-nine-year deal.

As it turns out, it was a ten-year agreement. I never saw
any checks for the single "Lookin' For Love" or the album
either, which had gone gold, because I didn't feel the need to
worry about it. I was always told by Cryer that my money was
being taken care of — being "put in my account," as Cryer
liked to say — and I was a trusting enough (not to mention
dumb enough) soul to believe whatever Cryer told me. According to him, I had everything comfortably squirreled away just
waiting on me whenever I needed it, including all of my record royalties and even my percentage of the money Gilley and
I were earning while we were on the road. Cryer said he was
taking care of it for me, and indeed he would give me a certain
amount of money per week, sort of like an allowance, so I
wouldn't spend it all, as he liked to say. From my point of
view, I never really had any reason to doubt the man because
to me, he seemed like a sharp businessman. After all, he had
taken that little lean-to shack and built it into the largest
beer joint in the world, complete with recording studio and
rodeo arena. I just couldn't argue with that kind of success. So
I rocked along for quite a while, feeling secure about myself
and Cryer for a long time.

I didn't find out about my true financial situation until
not long after Charlene Tilton and I married in 1982, when we
decided to buy a ranch in California. I went to Cryer and
asked for money from my account to close the deal on the
ranch. I figured there was so much in there by that time that
I could have probably bought the ranch for cash, considering
the gold records and albums I had been fortunate enough to
record. But Cryer just looked at me with those ice-blue eyes,
raised upright in the office chair he was sitting in, took his

hands from the bib of his overalls, and very calmly and coldly told me, "You ain't got no fuckin' money." It didn't even register at first. I thought he was joking.

But he wasn't. The money was just not there.

It was like falling off a cliff. I had been working every night for what seemed like forever, working big jobs too: Reno, Las Vegas, Lake Tahoe, and so on with Gilley. I always felt secure and never thought otherwise. I really thought my money would be taken care of by this guy who was like the dad that I never had. We went hunting and fishing together. We talked for hours about things, and he had a love for kids that you wouldn't believe. I thought he was a good man, having seen how often he would give new performers a chance in the club, or old-timers, on the skids, their one last shot at a chance to reach stardom again. But I should have seen through it when Charlene and I first got married and he told me he didn't want me to leave Texas. Gilley once told me after I signed a contract with Cryer, "Don't plan on going anywhere, because Sherwood has *ways*."

Cryer had people believing he was something like the Pasadena Mafia leader. One night he was mad at me for some reason or another, and the next thing I knew I was being jumped by a Pasadena police officer in the beer storage area at Gilley's. There was no way for me to fight back. He had a gun and a club, and if I had fought a policeman I could have easily been shot. I got out of it by acting like I was hurt. When you're a headlining performer at a club, and your good health means you'll be playing the next night and making the club money, you don't expect the boss at the club to arrange to have your head busted open.

Yeah, some people thought Cryer was a real godfather type. I discovered he was just a two-bit jerk.

So when I decided it was time to live somewhere else, after Cryer screwed me out of my money, he was very pissed. He said, "You'll never make it out of Texas. People in Texas are the only ones that like your music . . . you'll never make it in California or anywhere else." Looking back, I can see that he didn't want anyone to be independent; he wanted everyone to depend on him so that he could use them for profit. He even wanted Charlene and I to get married at Gilley's, ala the *Urban Cowboy* storyline, so he could make a big circus event out of it. But I put my foot down and said "No way," got my shit together, and moved to California.

After that, I hired some attorneys and filed on him for the money. When he got the papers he called me and said, "Hey, man, call the bird dogs off. This shit don't have to be like this . . . I'm gonna get it straight and make you a millionaire." He was always telling me he was going to make me a millionaire. Of course, with the success of *Urban Cowboy* and the music from it, I should have been one. At first I decided not to listen. But he kept talking until I made up my mind to give the son of a bitch another chance. I was still drawing a salary from Gilley's, though it was less than five hundred dollars a week, and I had stashed a little away on my own. But Cryer said he would have things straightened out in a couple of months.

Needless to say, it never changed. I finally got a lawyer and split from Sherwood Cryer. Unfortunately, my lawyer was in Los Angeles and couldn't practice in Texas, so he had to hire an attorney in Houston. Ironically, that attorney worked for Cryer in a lawsuit Gilley won against him just recently. When the dust settled, I had given up a Mercedes, my money, and most everything except the songs that I had written while under contract to him.

I was so mad that I wanted to put a shotgun in his mouth and smile as I pulled the trigger. And chances are if I hadn't had some responsibility in that I was married and had a little girl, I probably would have. I was never so devastated in my life. I'm still not over it, though I no longer am obsessed with the craziness of wanting to put a bullet in his head. I think I'm a bigger man than that.

Even though I wasn't legally split from Cryer until March 1986, I was away from him much earlier and was out on the road with my own act. The kick was, he owned In Concert, the booking agency that was booking me. I was with the William Morris Agency during the *Urban Cowboy* days, but Cryer pulled both me and Gilley out of William Morris and put us with his booking agency, though we had no idea at the time it was his booking agency. However, we still had some jobs that had been set up by William Morris which we were obligated to honor. The money from those jobs went to Sherwood Management, not Johnny Lee. Then Cryer never paid William Morris its commissions. So William Morris sued me and won, despite the fact that the agency knew Cryer was in charge of everything. I was so pissed off I never paid the bastards the $20,000 judgment.

So, by having control of the booking agency, he still had a lot of control over me. Naturally, my bookings slacked way off after we parted company. I couldn't afford to keep my band or my buses, and whatever else I had I lost.

Crisis:
Hurricane Charlene

Johnny's belief that Charlene Tilton was "Hollywood" personified may not have been far from the truth. Charlene was born on December 1, 1958, in San Diego but grew up in Hollywood. Just as Johnny knew all his life that he wanted to sing, Charlene knew what she wanted to do early on. From grade school on she was a performer. In high school she was, according to her biography from Lorimar, the president of the school's thespian club. Her credits as a professional actress skim over a career of a few commercials, including one spot in Japan at age fifteen with former Beatles drummer Ringo Starr for a line of clothing; bit parts in television shows; and movie credits that include *Freaky Friday* and the starring role in the motion picture *Big Wednesday* by age seventeen. That was all before landing the role of Lucy Ewing on the television series "Dallas." The part would bring her into most homes in America and in countries around the world through syndication.

So, when Johnny told his family he was marrying Charlene Tilton, everyone knew who he was talking about and some had their own opinion about how it would work. Johnny's mother and his Aunt Mary Lou, who probably knew him better than anyone,

73

had the most vocal opinions concerning Charlene and Johnny
and their marriage.

"I thought Charlene was as fine a person as she could be . . .
still do," says Mary Lou, "but she was too young and immature
to be married, and I thought their careers would conflict. The
one good thing that came out of it was Cherish."

Just after the birth of Cherish, Johnny's mother went to stay
with her son and his wife. She says she could feel a lot of tension
in the house, even though she and her daughter-in-law started
their relationship off amiably.

"Charlene and I just got along real well. I went out there
quite a bit, especially after Cherish was born. My husband and I
went out right after the baby came to help take care of her and
Charlene for a couple of weeks. And then when Johnny went on
tour in Europe, he called and I took time off from my job and we
went out and stayed with Charlene and Cherish . . .

"There were a lot of people there (after the baby was born)
and we finally talked with Charlene for a while . . . Then about
the time everyone started leaving, Johnny said something about
fixing a meal and, well, I knew Charlene wasn't in any condition
to do it, having just come home from the hospital. So, I walked
over and I asked her. 'Well, now, how do you feel about me, practically a stranger, just walking in and taking over your kitchen?'
She said, 'Hey, I think it's great . . . go right ahead.' And I guess
that broke the ice and we were real good friends.

"But I knew that the two of them would have a tough time
because their careers were so demanding. I even told Charlene
once, 'Now, this is going to be a hard old row to hoe here with
Johnny gone and you not able to go with him a whole lot because
of your career as well . . . do you think you're going to be able to
handle this?' And she said, 'Oh, yeah . . . no problem there . . .
everything's going to be great.' And, of course, I wanted everything to be good for them. But, unfortunately, it didn't turn out
that way."

Members of the family either saw the headlines in the su-
permarket tabloids or heard about them from friends almost con-
stantly. The stories started almost as soon as the whirlwind ro-
mance between the two stars heated up. Most of the people close
to Johnny, like his mother, discounted the stories — good, bad or
otherwise — as sensational gossip, designed to sell papers.

"You couldn't sneeze that they didn't write a story about it. However, the parts in the tabloids about Charlene's religion may have had some truth to them. In fact, I know her religion caused problems between them. I think, for a while, she got a little fanatic about the religion she was practicing. She had become a 'born again' Christian and decided to leave "Dallas" because she didn't want to do all of those bedroom scenes and wear revealing clothes. Johnny respected her convictions.

Like most people who go through a split-up, Johnny was devastated by his divorce with Charlene. His mother remembers how it affected her son: "He was very much in love with Charlene, and it took him quite a while to get over her leaving . . . and especially her leaving with Cherish and him not knowing where they were for so long."

"It was a stormy relationship," Aunt Mary Lou remembers, "and it always seemed to show up in one gossip sheet or another . . . So the whole thing was very sad, except, as I've said, the fact we have little Cherish in the world. Charlene does let us see her occasionally, and we do talk with her on the phone now that she's big enough. She's just grown up so quick . . . and she's just a sweet, pretty little girl."

Charlene upset the family early when she issued orders that there would be no pictures taken of Cherish, Johnny, or herself during the first family reunion after Cherish was born.

"She was just a spoiled little girl about the whole thing," Mary Lou remembers. "Here we were at a family reunion with cameras ready to take pictures of the new baby . . . and suddenly we couldn't. Charlene was just awful about it all. In fact, she hadn't told Johnny what she did and he was standing near me at one point, looking like he was ready to have his picture taken for the family album and I just stood there . . . He said, 'Aren't you going to take my picture?' I said, 'Well, I don't understand.' He said, 'What do you mean, you don't understand? We always take pictures and this is your only chance to get one of Cherish.' Then I said, 'Well, Charlene said not to take pictures . . . that you wouldn't allow it.' He got pretty upset at that.

"Later, I heard Charlene tell her agent or publicist on the phone that if any of us let those pictures out to the public, we would never hear the end of it from her. I was so hurt. I mean, we would have never done something like that. We all cared for

Johnny and his family. I tried to tell her that we wouldn't do something like that to them, and of course we never did, but she was very rude about it. Since then, the pictures have remained in my family album and have never been out of it. How she could have even thought that way I'll never know."

Johnny and Charlene at Cherish's first birthday party.

Charlene, Johnny, and Cherish came to honor Grandma Wilson, 1983.

6: Tabloid Marriage

I was once asked, concerning my marriage to Charlene Tilton, did anything ever go right? I doubt it. I think it was doomed from the beginning.

I was in love, or at least I thought I was. Perhaps infatuated would be more accurate. I know Charlene was in love. But it was with Hollywood, not me. In fact, everything with her was Hollywood, from the way she handled our marriage to the way she treated my family. She looked for publicity at every turn — good or bad, it was still publicity. And she and her PR people will tell you that any publicity is good publicity, no matter what it is or who it hurts. Sometimes I think she just married me for the publicity it would generate, because our marriage was one big publicity stunt for the tabloids to prey upon from the very beginning.

I once compared those types of newspapers to a bucket of manure: they stink to high heaven. Of course, if you leave shit alone, a crust forms over the top and it won't stink anymore. But if you stir it up again, it's going to stink again. I think the tabloids get their jollies — not to mention their readers — by stirring up the crap once it has crusted over so it'll continue to stink and sell papers at the grocery store checkout stand. It certainly works. Those papers have the highest circulation in the world, and the lowest regard for ethics, in my opinion.

As I said, my relationship with Charlene was in a fishbowl from the beginning. Charlene and I even met in the spotlight, at Dick Clark's celebration of the twentieth anniversary of "American Bandstand." I was sitting at the table with an old friend, Aaron Moran, who used to play Joanie on "Happy Days" and Charlene was just a couple of tables over with her live-in manager John Mercedes, the guy credited with discovering her. I had known of her from television and a few magazine articles I had read, and I was infatuated with her.

I went over to her manager and told him I had long before had a crush on Charlene and, without being disrespectful of his relationship with her, I wanted to meet her. So he introduced me to her. We talked for a few minutes, then she said something about wanting to meet Stevie Wonder, who was backstage at the time. I figured this would be a good way to score a few points with her and get her to myself for a while to talk, so I took her back. While we were backstage we hit it off just great and I wound up with her phone number. Well, naturally, I called her. We talked on a number of occasions. Although we were both pretty busy with our careers, it wasn't too long before we started dating.

I have to say that we had a lot of fun while we dated. We would meet at different places around the country, depending on where I was working and where she may be shooting. Mickey and I had an airplane and sometimes if she was going to be off for a while I'd go or send the pilot to pick her up. That was usually how we got to see each other between her shoots with "Dallas" or my schedule on the road with Mickey. Before long, Mercedes moved out and I just kind of moved in. Immediately we were an item, especially with the tabloids. Our schedules kept us busy, and there were times while we were dating that we didn't get to see each other very often. But apparently it was often enough, because one day she came home while I was taking a nap, woke me up, and said, "The doctor says I'm pregnant."

At the time there was no talk of marriage, though I wanted to get married and have the child, because I was serious about her and the baby. One night in my dressing room while playing at Vegas, I called Charlene and talked her into getting married. Thinking back, I remember she was more concerned about what it was going to do to her career on "Dallas" and how she would have to do things like shoot scenes standing behind furniture, so no one could tell she was pregnant.

The tabloids were publishing every kind of libelous story about us they could find. They would send people sneaking around, going through our trash to try to find things to write about. I mean, can you imagine digging through somebody's trash? Good Lord, I can think of some of the shit I threw out, just like everybody else does, and there ain't no way in hell I would put my hands in that stuff. Digging through people's garbage is nuts. But somebody, hard up for the money I guess, did just that and then gave it to these papers to make whatever out of it they could. It always amazed me how the tabloids would use terms like "reliable sources say . . ." until I later found out and Charlene admitted to my family that she and her press people had told the tabloids about one thing or another, making up a lot of it. Even more amazing, my own publicity people would release things to them without me knowing it; they thought that any publicity was good publicity. It got to where we couldn't even go grocery shopping without photographers everywhere taking pictures of us. I know I got tired of it. But it really bothered Charlene.

I remember when Charlene planned the wedding, we decided to get married out at Liza Minnelli's house at Lake Tahoe. Suddenly, Charlene's people wanted to hire all of these off-duty police officers as security to make sure the tabloids didn't get any photographs of the wedding. She was very secretive about everything, and was worried that the tabloids would ruin her career and ruin the marriage. They even had security people patrolling Lake Tahoe in boats, making sure the photographers couldn't get close enough to take any pictures. We ended up having a small wedding with some friends on Valentine's Day 1982 — and, lo and behold, no tabloid photographers. I did a concert that night at Lake Tahoe, then we spent our honeymoon there.

During that whole time between the wedding and the birth of our daughter, Cherish, the following August, Charlene didn't stay home much. Of course, a good bit of the time she spent shooting "Dallas," and watching out so her stomach didn't show on camera. And she was also taking singing lessons, which I thought was funny since they didn't help. She spent a lot of time and money on voice lessons and still couldn't sing. I mean, some people can, and some can be taught, then there are those who simply *can't sing*. She even made a record over in Europe called *C'est La Vie,* but no one ever played it. Besides that, I was always supportive of whatever she wanted to do. I'm just not sure she knew what she wanted.

To put it simply, the marriage just didn't work out. The only thing that did was Cherish.

She and my wife now, Debbie, are my life. From the minute Cherish was born she and I were inseparable. I helped the doctor deliver her and even helped them clean her up after delivery. The first night in the hospital she wouldn't stop crying, so I tried to calm her. Finally, I just picked her up and lay down on the bed that I had arranged for me to have in Charlene's room. I curled up around the baby and she immediately stopped crying. That's a feeling a father can't explain to anyone, and doesn't have to explain to another father. To this day my little girl and I are very, very close. But Cherish was another tabloid target.

They offered Charlene and I thousands of dollars and a new Mercedes and all kinds of things just for pictures. I said "No." Plain and simple. Still, we had to hire guards to stay at Charlene's room while she was still in the hospital so no one would take pictures and sell them to the tabloids.

Don't get me wrong. I wanted the whole world to know I had a beautiful little baby girl. I just wasn't going to let those blood-sucking bastards get the picture, much less insult us with the offer of money. Too much of my life was spent earning money; my baby would not become part of that madness. But, as usually happened with things like that, Charlene went too far with it.

When we went back to Texas for a family reunion, I later learned that she had told my family there would be *no* pictures of the baby or of her, for no reason. Now, my family is probably no different from any other family, especially when there's a new baby around. We take pictures at our get-togethers all the time and look back on them years later with pride and joy. Charlene said she just didn't want someone taking a picture of Cherish and selling it to the tabloids, which was the most ridiculous thing I had ever heard. My family would never do something like that. Those are the greatest people on earth (though I may be just a little bit prejudiced), and they have never tried to take advantage of me or my good fortune. Hell, if anyone was to walk in on a family get-together at my folks' place, they'd be hard-pressed to tell which one was a country singer and which one was a plant worker. We're all just family. What they would be able to tell is how much we love each other . . . and how many damn pictures we take when we're together! So when Charlene tried to put a stop to pictures, I put a stop to her bullshit.

I'm not sure how successful Charlene would have been anyway. I mean, you just try to tell a grandmother or an aunt who helped raise the father of the child that they can't take a picture of the baby. You'd have more hell on your hands than God's wrath from heaven, I'll guarantee it.

Pictures of the baby, pictures of me and Cherish, and pictures of my family and Cherish were taken — and not a one has ever left the family album. I knew they wouldn't. Charlene was more concerned about pictures of herself being leaked to the tabloids, and neither of us ever cared to grace the covers of those papers. I simply have no use for them.

The only time I got a real kick out of the tabloids was once while I was at home watching television. The commercial for one of the tabloids came on the screen with the "Inquiring minds want to know" spot showing my face and hands on a cartoon body in a cartoon drag line crane. I was lifting a cartoon lady with Charlene's face on it and dropping it on a pile of trash as the announcer sensationally screamed, "Johnny Lee drops Charlene Tilton!!!" I thought that was the funniest damn thing I had ever seen in my life. I don't know where they came up with the idea I was dumping Charlene, but I have to admit, it was hilarious. But, of course, it was very serious to Charlene. She was outraged. And she was on the phone screaming at people in no time. I don't know what she hoped to accomplish by jumping down someone's throat on the phone. I just learned to laugh those things off, though it didn't always laugh off so easily.

One time a tabloid headline read something like "Johnny Lee Drags His Dogs Through Beverly Hills On a Chain at 40 Miles Per Hour." What actually happened was, our dogs got into some mud near the edge of the pond we had on our place. At the same time our neighbors down the road were dressed up to go somewhere. Well, somehow the dogs got loose. Now, these were a couple of stupid ol' lap dogs. They didn't hurt anyone; they just got excited when they saw someone, thinking it was time to play. I got them for Charlene because she decided one day that she just had to have those damn dogs. I usually enjoyed them because they were playful, but on this particular day, I was wishing they were someone else's. Once they got out of the fenced-in area we had built for them, they ran down the street and playfully jumped up on the neighbors, getting them all muddy and wet. The neighbors called, raising all manner of hell, which I didn't blame them for. I calmed them down, apologized, said I would be right down to get the dogs, and even offered to replace the clothes the dogs had messed up. (Of course, the dogs had jumped up on their finest evening wear.)

Well, the situation was embarrassing enough when I got down there, but after seeing the dogs I sure as hell didn't want them in my car. So I put them on a leash, rolled the window down, and very slowly drove back up the road, almost at a snail's pace, holding the leash outside the window. No one saw me do this, but it ended up in the tabloids that I had dragged those poor animals back at forty miles per hour.

I didn't let it bother me too much. In fact, I joked about it at a concert soon thereafter. I told the audience that the paper had the story wrong. I said, "What actually happened was . . . I went down to the Society for the Prevention of Cruelty to Animals and asked them what would happen to all of their dogs if no one adopted them. And they sadly told me that eventually they would have to be destroyed. Well, I told them that wasn't going to be. So I got all of them — all forty or fifty of them — and tied them to the bumper on the rear end of my car. Now, I didn't go forty miles per hour, I went about fifty — all the way home through the streets of Beverly Hills. When I got home there were three dogs that made it, and I knew they would be good dogs so I kept them." Everybody at the concert got a good laugh out of the stupid story. But at the next concert we did, a bunch of people from the SPCA were picketing outside.

Anyone who saw me tell that story would have known I was joking. I love dogs. But there again, most people believe what they want to believe and hear what they want to hear. I think the combination of the tabloids and the nature of people to sift out the part they like the best is the recipe for career-ending rumors and sensational headlines. There's no accounting for what people will do just from reading stuff in the tabloids. I thought it was so bizarre that I made a joke of it. The real kick in the butt was when I found out that Charlene had called the tabloids with the story in the first place, telling them she was a neighbor. When I think back on it, that makes sense. After all, she was the only one who saw the incident.

A lot of things were written that were just unbelievable. Things like me beating Charlene. All you would have to do is look at the size of my big hand and the size of her small face to realize that the lies about me hitting her in the head — especially the stories of me hitting her fifteen or twenty times — were not even possible. That kind of beating would have killed a person of that size.

Questions were answered for me when I found out she and her press people were calling a lot of the time. There were articles about stuff that only she and I knew about, like an argument or a conversation we might have had. But she wasn't the only one. Sometimes people I thought were good friends would leak things to those papers. I might confide in a person and tell him something that may be bothering me — say, for example, that Charlene and I were not seeing eye to eye on something or that I thought she was being unreasonable about something. The next thing I knew, it would turn up in the papers, almost word for word, except where the paper thought it could "add" a little dialogue to make it better. I wonder sometimes, when people read that stuff, if they ever think about what it would feel like to see their most intimate thoughts or their most personal arguments with their spouse in print — then find out the spouse or even "best friend" provided it to the papers. Maybe they would reconsider what they read.

As much as it may sound like it, I'm not blaming the tabloids for all of the problems Charlene and I had. But the whole thing — the marriage, the publicity, all of it — just got to the point of being ridiculous.

When we first met, she loved what I did. She'd come with me to some concerts, though most of the time she was filming and couldn't get away to travel on the road. But toward the end, Charlene changed. She didn't like what I did anymore. She said I was always gone and wasn't a good husband. It was true that I was gone a lot, but that's what I did, just like filming "Dallas" or special shows was her career. It hurt me because nannies took care of Cherish when I had to go out on the road. It wasn't at all like a family.

Also, Charlene started going to a church that, before long, seemed to take her life over. She became what she called "born again" and started saying that was why she was against everything I was doing. But if she'd been serious about being a Christian, I don't think she would have acted the way she did. I was glad she was a Christian; I'm a Christian too. But this was different. She was almost using this thing about being "born again" as an excuse for her actions of hatred against me and everyone she was around, except the people in the church she went to. Then, all of a sudden, a lawyer from her church was advising her. The people in the church were telling her things that I believe made her think I was some kind of devil.

I'm not a theologian, but I was always taught that Christianity was based on love; that Jesus wants us to love everyone and to find the good in people. I know I'm not a saint, but I'm not the devil incarnate either. My wife Debbie knew me when I was at my lowest — out of steady work, with a poor self esteem. Yet she managed to find the love in me that she nourished and helped grow until I was a whole person again. She has never once yelled "born again" to me, but her love has made me feel like I had new life.

I'm not trying to put down people who say they're "born

again." I know what accepting Jesus is about — and it isn't about judging and being hateful to others. There isn't a day that goes by I don't look to the Lord and thank Him for my loving wife, my beautiful little girl, and my caring family and friends.

One day I came home early from a road tour to find a lot of bags and suitcases in the living room. Charlene said it was just some things she was getting rid of, so I didn't think anything about it. The next day I took one of the cars and went Christmas shopping. It was just a few days before Christmas, and I was loaded down with gifts for Charlene and Cherish. But when I walked in the door and put down the gifts, I noticed the quiet. I called out. No answer. I thought maybe they had gone out for a while, perhaps shopping or something. But as I looked around I noticed a lot of things were gone, things that Charlene used or wanted. I began to have a sick feeling in my stomach and my insides began to burn as I walked around that big house, discovering clothes missing and the baby's things nowhere in sight. As I started realizing what had happened, I could feel the tears in my eyes. They were hot as fire, and I couldn't stop them. I kept thinking there was some simple explanation that would prove my deepest fears wrong. And, in fact, there was a simple explanation: Charlene had taken Cherish and left. They were gone.

For several days I didn't know where they were. That's got to be the most helpless feeling in the world. Taking Cherish from me was like jerking my soul right out of my body. I'm not ashamed to say that I cried my eyes out wondering aloud where my baby was. I know it may sound funny that I was more concerned with my baby than my wife, but I was.

A couple of days later I had to do a concert at the Palomino Club. Ironically, they were filming me that night. I asked the audience if anyone had any requests and some guy pops up out of the crowd, comes to the stage, puts some papers in my hand, and leaves. I opened them only to discover I had been served with divorce papers in the middle of my show, on camera, right at Christmas time.

The next thing I knew, a police officer showed up at the house with a piece of paper saying I had to vacate the premises within twenty-four hours. Well, my God, there was no way I was going to be able to get all of my stuff out of the house that quickly. I called my friend Doc Harry, and he came to help. In fact, he let me move in with him in Redondo Beach, California. Doc and Cecil helped me when I needed it the most. When I left I took what I could of mine. I didn't take anything that belonged to Charlene, but I did take a couple of Cherish's baby pictures.

When it came time to go to court, my lawyer told me that half of everything was mine. But I made it clear then and there that I didn't want anything of hers — not her money or property or anything. I told Charlene I just wanted to see my baby. So, Charlene made me one promise — to never keep Cherish from me. She has since broken that promise. And every time I want to see my little girl, I have to go to the attorney and sign court papers. Every time.

Despite that, I see her as often as I can and call her almost every day. Charlene tells her it's her Daddy *Johnny* on the phone. That hurts. Hearing your child call you "Daddy" is priceless. I don't know how many times I've been feeling down and I would call and talk with Cherish, or she would come up to me and say "Daddy," and it would make me feel like the king of the world.

I'm supposed to have joint custody, which most divorced fathers know is the biggest joke ever played on a man. I'm entitled to have half the say-so in how she is brought up, but anyone who's gone through a divorce probably knows what joint custody really means. I still hope for the day when Cherish would want to come live with Debbie and me. I would love it, but I don't know if that will ever happen. I miss not being able to see her as often as I want.

I think Charlene, for the most part, rears Cherish all right — despite the incident of being arrested for driving while intoxicated when Cherish was in the car! I think that's one time I could have lived up to the claims of the tabloids and beat the ever living crap out of Charlene. When I think about the possibility that Charlene could have killed my little girl because she was driving drunk, I get enraged. Especially over the fact that she actually told Cherish "not to tell Daddy Johnny." Imagine, she wanted my daughter to lie to me. Of course, Cherish didn't lie to me. She told Debbie and me all about it.

I feel very strongly about people who drink and drive. Actually, I think if they want to kill themselves, to hell with them — let them do it. The problem is they could kill other innocent people in the car with them or on the road near them, so it just doesn't work to drink and drive. But I never became so impassioned about something until I learned that Charlene had been drinking and driving with my baby in the car. I think Miss Tilton learned a lesson. For Cherish's sake, I hope Charlene did.

During my years with Charlene, I met a lot of truly nice people. The people from "Dallas" — Larry Hagman, Victoria Principal, all of them — were so nice. But there were those who were into the Hollywood scene that I didn't care for very much. People who, when they talked to you, were already looking somewhere else for another famous face or someone to notice them. I don't know, I was raised a little differently. Where I come from you look at someone when you talk with them, and there just wasn't much of that going on out there.

It's true that many Hollywood types are shallow — not all, but many. I can't live that way. Anyone who knows me or has even just met me can usually tell how I feel. There's no bullshitting about me. But perhaps a lot of people in that scene are so shallow because of the publicity. Maybe I should have adopted their act. I guess I just didn't see any reason for it, which probably caused some of the negative publicity I received.

For example, my drinking. Any time I had a drink of anything in my hand — water *or* beer — when I took a sip . . . *snap . . . snap . . . snap . . .* the flashes on the cameras would start. Then, before you could blink, it was on the cover of a tabloid newspaper: "Johnny Lee's Drinking Problem." The Hollywood element was everywhere, from the parties we attended to the private disagreements that would strangely end up on the front page of a tabloid. All I know is, I never called them once.

Although I think highly of many of the people on

"Dallas," I don't watch the show. It's a fine show. I'm just not much of a soap opera watcher, whether during the day or at night. I had only seen the show a few times before I met Charlene. On the other hand, that was about the only show Charlene watched. She taped every episode and ran them over and over again. I'm not sure if she was trying to learn from them to better her performances in upcoming episodes, or if she just liked looking at herself on television.

The reason Charlene left "Dallas" was that she said her beliefs would not allow her to portray the type of character Lucy was on the show. She said she didn't feel her religious convictions would stand for her wearing what she felt were revealing clothes and doing bed scenes. Lorimar told her they didn't need her, since that's the character Lucy was scripted as. So, without further delay, she and Lorimar parted company. Before long, after she lost a bunch of weight, she went back and they finally hired her again. She still plays the same character, the show's still a nighttime soap opera full of intrigue and steamy scenes, so not much has really changed. I'm not sure what happened to her religious beliefs. I just hope it makes her a rich woman so she'll be able to afford to bring my little girl up right. Lord knows I pay my share, and not because I have to — because I want my little girl to be taken care of properly. Charlene's got her hands full as it is with her new husband, whom she met in Europe while we were still married.

I've been asked before if we ever cheated on each other. I can say with a clear conscience that I did not. Whether she did or not, I don't know — and I really don't care. All I know for a fact is that she met this fellow while we were still married. I don't know much about him except that he doesn't work. The last time we were in court over child support, it tickled me when my lawyer made a clear-cut point about that.

My lawyer had him on the stand and said, "Mr. Tilton . . . I . . . I mean, Mr. Allen, what do you do for a living?"

Allen says, "Well, I'm a singer and an actor."

My attorney then asked, "Well, in the last three months have you earned anything as an actor to contribute to the well being of your wife and Cherish?"

Allen said, "No."

"Well," my lawyer said, "what about during the last six months, have you earned any money as an actor?"

"No."

"Okay," my attorney says, "what about since you've known Ms. Tilton, have you earned anything as an actor that would contribute to the well being of your wife and Cherish?"

Allen sort of twisted around in his chair and looked away and said, "No."

"Fine, Mr. Allen," my lawyer said. "Now, what about your singing career? Have you earned any money during the past three months as a singer to contribute to the family?"

Allen, realizing the embarrassing line of questioning was going to begin again, looked helplessly to Charlene's attorney, who knew good and well the line of questioning was relevant and that he could not do anything but get overruled on objections.

"All right," my attorney finally said, "let's just quit messin' around with this. Have you ever made any money as an actor or singer since you've been married to Ms. Tilton?"

Allen said, "No, I have not."

My attorney then replied, "I see, then that means I could be an actor or a singer."

That pissed Allen off, but it made the point. Here they were trying to get $5,000 per month in *child support* when the guy Charlene was married to was living off of her money. I don't ever mind paying for my baby, but I do mind financing him.

As it turned out, there was a nominal increase in child support, something I would have agreed to from the beginning. But greed got in their way.

I face this kind of thing from time to time, when they want to mess with my mind. One particular episode was brought on when Debbie and I kept Cherish for a couple of extra days at Christmas. We had a great time. The families came over and Santa gave Cherish a lot of toys. We had a real big family Christmas dinner. I couldn't have asked for a better Christmas, and Cherish and Debbie were the best Christmas presents I could have asked for. So, when it came time to take Cherish back, it was kind of rough.

Once we were at the airport, to take Cherish back to

Charlene, Cherish started crying. She didn't want to go back. She had been loved the whole time by families that really cared for her, and the thought of going back made her feel very sad. I guess most kids are like that, especially at Christmas time when they get to visit with their grandparents and the home is filled with joy and laughter. So, naturally, Cherish began to cry and hold onto us while we were at the airport waiting for the flight. That got Debbie to crying, and I was even crying. I can handle a lot, but not watching my little girl cry when she has to leave us. So I said, "This is a bunch of bull. She's not in school, why does she have to go back right now?"

Well, I called and told Charlene I was going to keep her a couple of extra days. It was the first Christmas I had spent with her since she was born. She had had a great time and really wanted to stay a couple of extra days longer. There seemed to be no problem with that whatsoever. We agreed on a new time when she would meet us at the airport, and I got all three of our reservations changed for a couple of days later.

But when we arrived at the airport with Cherish a couple of days after that, at the agreed upon time, Charlene was there with her new husband and her lawyer to serve me with papers to go to court for having kept her longer than I was supposed to. Well, of course, the court wouldn't even hear it because the accusation was so utterly ridiculous. But it was the only way they could get back at me.

When I think about it, it's a shame that people have to be that way, because they know I would do anything for Cherish, including lay down my life for her. Still, if occasionally going to court and signing a few papers when I want to see her is what I have to do, so be it.

The only thing I worry about is the effect it may have on Cherish. She's beginning to understand things, and I worry about it making her bitter or resentful. I pray to God that she never thinks a day in her life that I never wanted to see her or be with her. One of the reasons I don't seek custody is because of what it would more than likely put Cherish through. It's an arduous process that no child should ever have to endure. Besides, I promised Charlene I would never do that, and despite the promises she has broken, I will do everything I can to keep my word.

As I said before, the one occasion when I almost sought custody was the time Charlene was arrested for DWI. I was beside myself, I was so mad. Cherish actually had to go to jail while Charlene was booked. The police had to take care of her until someone could go and get her.

Debbie and I were furious when we found out about that.

The whole ordeal — our marriage, the split-up and divorce — had its effects on my family. At the time I wasn't in close contact with my family, being so far from home and traveling as much as I did. So most of the time they would hear about everything through the grapevine before I had a chance to tell them. In fact, what probably affected them most was having friends and acquaintances who would read about something in a tabloid then run into one of the members of my family and say, "Hey, heard about Johnny," or "Saw something about Johnny and Charlene in the paper, what's the inside story on that?" I think that bothered them more than anything.

But I would try to make light of it, even joke about it with my uncles and tell my mom and my aunts, "Now, just don't pay attention to that stuff." They didn't duck their heads in shame or anything, because they also knew that I thought it was the biggest damn joke there was. But I know it probably bothered them. My family loves me, and they knew what I was going through, especially with the divorce. I mean, when a grown man bows up and cries because his baby was taken from him, a family hurts with him. Even Charlene called my Aunt Mary Lou after the divorce and apologized for some of the things in the tabloids, and even admitted that she or her press people had reported some things.

Charlene's mother even got in on the act, writing terrible letters to me, calling me everything she could think of, and demanding I stay away from Charlene and Cherish. I saved the letters, and I told Charlene that if she was telling Cherish the wrong things, then someday I would give Cherish the letters to show her the way her grandmother treated me and my family.

A lot has been made over Charlene's religion at the time. Some have even referred to it as a cult. It wasn't a cult. She needed something at the time and turned to a church. A lot of people do that. I have done that. I find the church and my beliefs to be a strength to me, especially when I'm going through rough times. It's really a personal thing that only the person involved can determine: Is the answer at church or simply in seeking God? So, I don't really know what Charlene's decision to begin going to church was based on. I don't need to know, because that's her business.

The only thing that bothered me about it all was the way she pushed it on me — then tried to use it against me. For example, I don't need to do aerobics to gospel music to reinforce my beliefs, but if that's what she wanted to do, then fine. However, when some of her newfound *Christian* friends in the church began to persuade her in certain ways, especially against me, then I felt like she had crossed the line. I could see what was going on. I may be a country boy, but I'm not stupid.

I mean, imagine the lawyer from her church who offered his services for free. Who was he trying to kid? There isn't a lawyer on earth who does anything for free. I know; I've paid a lot of money to a lot of lawyers, usually for nothing more than sitting on their asses and making a phone call or two. This fellow saw a chance to make a name for himself. After all, he was representing a big television actress from a very popular TV show against a gold record country music singer. Either way you slice it, he was in it for the profit or notoriety. He had it set up so I had to go through him to see my daughter. Christian charity? Give me a break.

No, I don't think Charlene was involved in any kind of cult, but I wonder about the advice she got. I don't think that's what a church is all about. I always thought a church tried to help keep the family together, not let it — or even help it — fall apart.

People have asked whether this was a marriage for the sake of Hollywood — "two stars meet and fall in love," that type of thing. From my perspective it wasn't; from hers, I'm not sure. I know it took a while to talk her into marrying me, though there was never talk of not having the baby. Whether it was someone's bright publicity idea that changed her mind remains to be seen. But after the marriage it was definitely a wall-to-wall publicity party.

Although this hasn't been easy for Debbie to handle, she's done a remarkable job with it and has stood by me every step of the way since we met in the summer of 1985. Unfortunately, some people forget or simply don't pay attention to what they're saying and will ask about Charlene or what happened between Charlene and me — while Debbie is standing there. Sometimes it upsets her, and I don't blame her. She knows it's my past, and she knows she's my future. But sometimes after several people walk up at a party or golf tournament and say, "Hey, yeah, Johnny Lee . . . weren't you married to Charlene Tilton?" she'll just have to unload. Even friends of ours will hear about something Charlene has done and ask me if I've heard about it. Sometimes when we're alone after remarks about Charlene have been made, Debbie will say, "Why don't they just let it end? I don't really care about what Charlene has done." I understand how she feels. I listen and I talk with her, and we work it out.

That's the reason our marriage is working. We work it out, no matter what it is. After a while, it gets easier to work things out, I guess because we understand each other better every day. And perhaps because we know how the other person feels and do what we can to make each other feel loved.

But as far as my ex-wife is concerned, Debbie knows it's almost a given that Charlene will be brought up in conversation from time to time. She doesn't particularly like it, and she'll probably never get over it, but she handles it. And I figure if she can, then so can I.

Resurrection:
Debbie and Johnny

Since their relationship began in 1985, Debbie Lee has seen some of the changes that have been going on in her husband's life from a perspective no one else ever has, including ex-wife Charlene. When Debbie married Johnny, he was sliding fast into the oblivion of country music "has-beens." The lack of concern by managers for his career growth and the devastating blows of a celebrity divorce played out before the world had toppled him from the peak of stardom. He was tumbling painfully down the mountain, with no chance of surviving the fall, when Debbie entered his life and caught him before he hit bottom.

"Johnny is a very giving person," says Debbie, a former airline attendant and model, "but it seemed as if almost everyone wanted to take advantage of him. He would give you the shirt off his back. In fact, when he traveled to, say, Lake Tahoe or Vegas, he would many times give money to the guys in the band to go gamble with or just have fun with . . . no mention of paying it back. He just wanted them to have fun and be able to relax. I think he remembers what it was like to be without money despite how hard you work."

But sometimes, despite his goodwill, problems would arise.

"Right after we got married," Debbie recalls, "we were on

the road. And I had become friends with Ed, one of the guys in the band. He was a good friend of Johnny's. We would sit and talk while Johnny signed autographs after the show. Sometimes we would talk for a couple of hours because Johnny would always stay as long as someone wanted to talk with him or have him autograph something. Now, Johnny had done a lot for this guy. He had given him custom-made clothes, money . . . really taken care of him when he needed help . . .

"At the same time, Johnny and I, like a lot of newlywed couples, had a few little problems. Nothing serious, just typical things that two people usually have to work out. But I had noticed that we seemed a little distant from each other . . . and so had Ed. Keep in mind, when you travel for long periods of time in close proximity like that, you become like family and it's sometimes hard to keep things from showing. So if Johnny and I were disagreeing about something, rather than try to help like a real friend would, or even just decide to keep his nose out of our personal business, Ed would, for some reason, prey on our problems. I still don't know why he suddenly turned on Johnny like he did, but he did."

The incidents began on a five-day road trip that Debbie had missed. One night Johnny returned to the bus after a lot of drinking and got into another bunk, not his own in the stateroom. In the meantime, Ed brought a girl into the stateroom. After the tour ended, Ed told Debbie about the girl on the bus — except he said it was Johnny who brought her on and took her to the stateroom.

"Naturally, I was upset, and I wanted to find out what happened. So, I made up a story about some girl claiming to have pictures of what went on that night and I confronted Johnny with it later while we were traveling on the bus. Well, Johnny went back to the rear of the bus to talk with the guys to find out what was going on. A short time later, while he was still back there, Ed came out and said Johnny was upset and didn't know what to tell me . . . The fact of the matter was, Johnny was upset because all during the time the girl was on the bus, he was asleep in another bunk and didn't even know the incident had happened. In fact, he wasn't in the back of the bus wondering what to do. That was just another lie this guy had made up. Now the whole thing was getting all twisted up. I got upset and decided I needed a few days away, so I went to Dallas."

While she was in Dallas, Debbie got a call from Ed. He said that following the show that evening, Johnny had taken a girl to one of the other guys' room — afraid that Debbie might suddenly show up and catch them. She called his room and found that the whole band was having a party after the concert in somebody else's room.

"I waited until the tour was over before I told him about it, because I knew he would probably kill the guy if I'd told him while they were on the road and I was in Dallas," Debbie remembers. "When I did tell him, he was furious. He confronted the band leader about it, and they decided to fire Ed.

"Most people would tend to get hard after that, to build a wall around themselves. Not Johnny. In fact, we began to grow closer as he learned that I did trust him and that I did and still do love him. I wanted to know what really happened, but I gave him the benefit of the doubt . . . and I was right. It was also a growing experience for me."

Debbie says it was hard to get used to the ladies who would come up after the shows to hug and kiss her husband.

"I remember the first time I went with him to a show after we were dating . . . the lines of girls, one kiss right after the other. I couldn't believe it. I could see what the attraction was, obviously, especially since he was a celebrity. However, I got my point across to him later that night.

"I just walked out to the bus while he kissed these girls, and waited for him. When he finally came out, he brought me a yellow rose that some other girl had given to him, and believe it or not, he wanted to give it to me. So, he reached over to kiss me and I turned my face away and he said, 'What are you doing?' I laughed at him and said, 'I'm not kissing you. Go back there and wash your face first.' I think I got my point across to him that there are other ways of giving yourself."

One of the toughest things Debbie had to learn to handle was the notoriety of her husband's past, in particular, his marriage to Charlene Tilton.

"At first it was tough because she and Johnny were so closely associated with each other in the public's eye. Sometimes he'll be somewhere, some show or golf tournament, and there will be an old biography in the program, for example, that may say something about his marriage to Charlene. As a matter of fact, right after we were married we were at the Doug Kershaw

Golf Tournament and the program had an old bio listing Charlene Tilton as his former wife, rather than the fact that he and I
are now married. Johnny was furious . . . We went to the tournament director, who apologized profusely. But the thing that put
everything into perspective was when Joanna Kerns, star of
"Growing Pains," came up to me during lunch and told me that if
it were her she would have it retracted, because she felt Charlene was no asset to Johnny. Now this told me what the people in
Charlene's own industry thought of her . . . From that point on I
never had difficulty handling the fact that Johnny was once
married to Charlene, partially because everyone had this opinion of her."

Debbie was right about what the people in Tilton's business
thought of her. Actor Gary Culver had worked with the cast of
"Dallas" during the first three episodes of the show when it
began production in 1977.

"Charlene was strictly Hollywood," Culver recalls. "She
didn't have anything to do with those of us who were not the reg-
ulars on the show, and not much more to do with the main players. Folks like Larry Hagman and Linda Grey were very kind.
They seemed to enjoy themselves and treated those of us who
had small parts just as they treated anyone else. They were
professional in every way. But Charlene, she was a different
story. I really couldn't get to know her as well as the other cast
members, because she was just too snobby."

Dallas Times-Herald television critic Bob Brock thinks it
wasn't so much Tilton being a snob as it was Tilton just not
being mature enough in the business to know how to act around
other actors. "Her uncertainty," he says, "perhaps made her that
way." Brock remembers the only interview he ever did with Tilton as "basically a forgettable interview." The critic chuckles
when he thinks back on the question-and-answer session with
Tilton during her first full season on "Dallas."

"I remember her agent, John Mercedes, as sort of a svengali.
He controlled the interview and basically pulled the strings for
her answers . . . Despite that, and reflecting on it years later, I
come away with the feeling that she sort of had a determination
to succeed. I recall she did seem like a real survivor. Whether
she has grown up any over the years, I don't really see any. They
still don't really have much for her to do on "Dallas," and I
wouldn't suggest she sell the farm and go it on her own . . . She

just doesn't seem to have any great charisma. There's nothing
that sets her apart."

As far as the way Tilton was toward Johnny, Debbie received a good education.

"I had learned a few things about her while Johnny and I
were dating because of some of the nasty things she did. Johnny
had given me her address because of Cherish. There were specific things Cherish would ask for that Johnny and I wanted to
send her. Cherish and I are very close, she's like my own daughter, and I had sent her things she had wanted when she would
visit us. I found out that when they would arrive and Charlene
would open them only to find out they were from me, she would
box them back up and return them to Johnny, refusing to give
them to Cherish because she didn't want to confuse her as to who
her real mother is.

"Cherish and I know each other very well. We get along
wonderfully, and love each other more than anyone could know.
She also knows that I'm very important to her daddy . . . but we
always made sure she knew who her real parents were. Still,
that kind of thing didn't seem to be as important to her as how
much we cared about her. And as far as we're concerned, caring
for Cherish is the easiest and most natural thing in the world.
It's not hard to love a little angel."

When Cherish started calling Debbie "Mommy," Charlene
was enraged. Debbie found it to be a tender situation.

"Once, Cherish and I were on a plane flying her back to
Charlene from a visit, and I noticed she had a little eyelash on
her cheek. When I took it off, she got real excited and wanted to
make a wish. Apparently, she likes to play a little game where
when she loses an eyelash she makes a wish and blows it from
her little hand. So, I held her eyelash while she made a wish and
blew. Then I asked her, 'What's your wish?' She said, 'To be able
to call you Mommy.' I said, 'Sweetheart, I'd love for you to call
me Mommy.' But she said Charlene wouldn't let her . . . even
though Charlene had insisted she call her husband 'Daddy.' So,
Johnny explained to her quite simply that he was her 'real
daddy.' Now Cherish understands everything very well. The only
one who has ever confused her is Charlene."

Charlene and Debbie had begun, over time, to establish an
amiable relationship and would talk with each other over the
phone, especially about Cherish. But on one Christmas Day it

would be different. Cherish was with Johnny and Debbie for the holidays for the first time. Charlene had tried to call several times, but the lines were busy with Christmas calls. Then the next time she called, Cherish was taking a nap. Debbie told Charlene she would have Cherish call her when she woke up, but the minute Cherish got up she wanted to ride her new bicycle. Soon after that Charlene called again.

"I told her that Cherish was riding her bicycle but that I would see if they were nearby," Debbie recalls. "Well, I walked outside and couldn't see them, so I called, but they were gone. I went back in and picked up the phone and told Charlene that they were still gone but that I would have Cherish call her the minute she got back. All of a sudden Charlene began cursing at me. I couldn't believe it. I had been as nice as I could to this lady and now she was cursing at me . . . and on Christmas Day, no less. So, I hung up the phone.

"I couldn't help remembering the times . . . countless times . . . we had called Cherish and she wouldn't let us talk with her or she would have the answering machine on and not pick up the phone."

That was the same Christmas visit that Johnny and Debbie asked for a few extra days with Cherish, got permission from Tilton, and were subsequently ordered to court when they did arrive as they had all agreed. But that wasn't the only holiday visit that ended in a hassle. On another Christmas visit, a miscommunication caused a great deal of confusion and hard feelings.

"The night before we were to fly Cherish back from her Christmas visit with us, Charlene's attorney called, her attorney mind you, to get the flight information. I was waiting on a call from Johnny's agent and didn't have the information at my fingertips, so the attorney just suggested I call and leave the information on Charlene's answering machine. So, as soon as I had talked with Johnny's agent, I called Charlene's number and I left very specific instructions on her answering machine as to the flight number, when we would arrive, and to meet us at the US Air ticket counter. I made it clear to meet at the ticket counter because our turnaround flight would leave shortly thereafter and we would need to be able to check in quickly to make our return flight. We always fly with Cherish to pick her up or take her home. She feels better when Johnny and I are with her, and for that matter, so do we.

"When we arrived at the airport, no Charlene. So we waited and waited; still no sign of Charlene. Finally, when they announced the final boarding call for our flight back home, Johnny looked at me and said, 'Come on, we're taking her back home.' And we did.

"The minute we got off the plane from the flight back, they were paging us. Charlene was on the phone, screaming at Johnny, 'Get back on that plane! Bring Cherish home . . . Debbie's instructions weren't clear and you weren't there when we got there!' Johnny said, 'Look, this isn't our fault. You had the instructions on your answering machine, and we're not getting back on that plane.' Then she told Johnny to just put Cherish on the plane and send her back alone. Johnny said, 'Look, Charlene, if she doesn't want to fly alone I'm not making her.' So, Charlene wanted to talk to her, and when Cherish got on the phone the child began to cry uncontrollably because Charlene was telling her she had to fly back alone. I knelt down beside her and said, 'Give me the phone, honey,' and I put the receiver to my mouth and told Charlene, 'That's enough!' I gave Johnny the phone and took Cherish over to some seats in the terminal to calm her down. She was horrified of flying alone and thought she would have to get on the plane by herself . . . and Charlene was going to make her!

"Johnny said, 'Charlene, you get on a plane and come get Cherish. She's not flying alone and we're not taking her back tonight.' The child had been on a plane most of the day, it seemed.

"When we got back home Charlene called, and I didn't even get a chance to say hello before she was apologizing. She said, 'I'm very sorry, Debbie. You were right. I rewound the message and listened to it again and you did leave the right instructions.' I told her that I accepted her apology and left it at that.

"Charlene did come to get Cherish the next day. And it just broke my heart when she arrived and Cherish grabbed onto my leg and didn't want to leave. She started crying and Charlene had to peel her off my leg telling her, 'Come on, Cherish, we have to go,' and it just killed me to see that. When Cherish is with us she wants to live with us, and she and I have grown very close. But they make it so hard for us to see her, and they tell her things that hurt us."

Debbie says she doesn't understand some of the things Charlene gets upset about. For instance, when Johnny and Debbie

gave Cherish a "Sheera, The Princess of Power" doll that she
wanted, Charlene immediately grabbed it from her.

"She told that little girl that things like that are satanic,"
Debbie said. "First of all, I don't think children of that age understand words like 'satanic.' And besides, Cherish knows God
loves her, and looks forward to things like church and saying her
prayers. All she knows is that "Sheera" is a character who does
good, and I think little girls, just like little boys, should have
characters like that that they can relate to as being good and
moralistic . . .

"The irony lies in the fact that Charlene would profess such
high moralistic standards, but she was the one who was arrested
for driving drunk . . . and with Cherish in the car! Johnny and I
were absolutely beside ourselves! To think what could have happened . . . it scared us to death! And to make matters worse she
told Cherish not to say anything to us about it. Well, of course
she told us about it. We talk about everything. If she has something on her mind, we talk about it like buddies."

Debbie believes that Johnny and Charlene had problems because Tilton didn't fully understand Johnny.

"Charlene was once quoted as saying she never had any control over Johnny . . . which is probably true. That alone answers
a lot of questions about why their marriage didn't work out. To
be married to someone doesn't mean you control them. Johnny
and I appreciate each other, and that's very important. It may
sound corny, but sometimes I can't believe how much in love we
are. And when you love someone that much, you respect them.
You let them be themselves, and in turn they will be good to you
and for you.

"Johnny has been so good to me . . . he's just a super person.
It's usually the little things that really mean so much to me, because the little things he does for me are so special. We've had
our problems, but we've learned to lean on one another. He and I
put one another first. His career is important, obviously, but
we've found that we belong together and so we take care of each
other because that's even more important."

Debbie says some of the things they have gone through, including the death of their child, Heaven, have brought them
even closer together.

She is probably the best "manager" Johnny has ever had.
Knowing him so well, she can usually anticipate what's going to

happen and keep him on track, while lending the support of a loving wife.

"The Johnny I met is a lot different from the Johnny I know now," she explains. "He was doing things that many times I didn't approve of, but I never pressured him. For so many years, he had no guidance . . . there was no one for him to answer to, but that's because he's his own person. What I try to do is keep him on schedule and not let him worry about the details so much, so he can concentrate on his singing and his shows. Johnny has an artistic form that needs to be free.

"It all goes back to a time while he was still legally tied to Sherwood Cryer. I had noticed his road managers would seem to always keep him upset. To me that seems stupid, because if Johnny's upset, then the band is upset and that means they don't function right, which in turn means he doesn't function right and no one is happy. So I watched the way things were handled for a long time, about two years to be exact. Then I began to take care of a few minor things for him. I had to take it slow, because Johnny had never allowed a woman into that small circle with him. He didn't really know how our relationship would work if I was also in the capacity of planning things with him. But he's allowed me to do a little at a time, and by doing this he's seen how much easier it made things for him. After all, he and I know very well that there's no one else in this world who wants to help him any more than I.

"Sure, a road manager is hired to do a job, but not his wife. More than anyone else, I want to see him succeed . . . more than anyone else, I want to see him happy. And I've learned what it takes to do that. I watched all the mistakes that were made and I learned the right things to do, to the point that I can anticipate his needs and concerns and have most of them taken care of before he even asks or they ever arise. I do it because Johnny's always been the type of person to take one day at a time. He doesn't want to think about planning anything later on in his life, which is fine. So I try to keep things simple and organized. I'm not doing it for me or for him . . . I'm doing it for us."

"I did." Johnny and Deb's wedding, November 14, 1986, Maui, Hawaii.

Mr. and Mrs. Johnny Lee

"Doc" Harry, Deb, Johnny, Julie Crenshaw, and Chris.

At Vegas, to see Jerry Lee Lewis and Fats Domino on Debbie's twenty-seventh birthday.

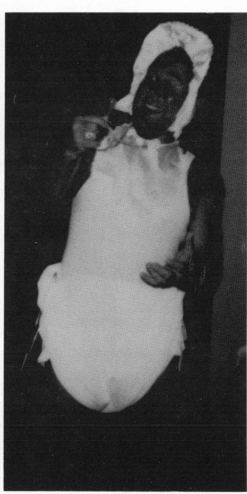

"I over married."

"I dressed up like this and met Deb at the airport in Tucson, when we found out she was pregnant."

Johnny, Debbie, and Cherish, Christmas, 1987.

Christmas 1987. From left: Lynn, Paul (top), Johnny, Mom, Jimmy, Joyce, and Cherish and Deb in front.

At the 1986 Doug Sanders Tournament.

Johnny and Cherish, July Fourth at Aunt Mary Lou's, 1984.

Cherish "Cow Punk" Lee, 1988.

Cherish and Debbie, 1989.

Aunt Mary Lou, Johnny, and Debbie at the Houston Hotel, 1987.

Jody Davis, Dale Earnhardt, Debbie, Johnny, and Walt Garrison, 1988.

Forty-third birthday.

"Which one is the dummy?"

Johnny and his buddy Uncle Charles at Memorial Park golf course in Houston, 1986.

Johnny's caddy, Travis, with Johnny, Debbie, Bubba, and Marlene. Doug Sanders Tournament, 1988.

"My family." (Back) Jimmy Wilson, Billy Wilson, Gene Wilson; (middle) Mary Lou Wilson and Virginia Wilson; (bottom) Grandma Claudia Wilson and Grandpa Wilson.

Johnny and Grandma Wilson had a birthday party together in 1974.

Grandma Wilson holding Cherish Lee for the first time, 1983.

Brothers and sisters: (left to right) Janice, Claudia, Jimmy, Lynn, Janes, and Johnny. Mother (Virginia Callier) is in back.

Paul, Mom, Grandma Wilson, Uncle Billy, Aunt Hazel, and Aunt Mary Lou, 1983.

Billy Wilson, Jimmy Wilson, Grandma Claudia Wilson, and mother, Virginia, 1975. Aunt Mary Lou is absent in this picture of people who cared for Johnny while he was growing up.

Uncle Billy Wilson, Aunt Mary Lou Miller, and Johnny's mother, Virginia Callier, 1986.

Uncle Billy just got his farming license, 1989.

Johnny and Mom, 1982.

Mom, 1986.

Johnny and his mom (left) with Aunt Mary Lou and Uncle Charles, 1982.

7: Breath of Life

Debbie and I had met a couple of times before the day I asked for her phone number. The first time I was traveling with my road manager, Terry Reinhart, and Debbie was a flight attendant on our flight. When she started to serve us, Terry introduced himself and told her who I was. Debbie seemed to think he was flirting or something, using my name to introduce himself. I don't remember meeting her on that flight; we must have said no more than hello to each other. Then, when I was on the road with Gilley, Debbie's friends took her to our concert at a college in Martin, Tennessee. She told me later that she thought I was cute and wanted to meet me. She got a "Lookin' For Love" T-shirt at the concert, but we never talked with each other.

As fate would have it, years passed until one day, in June 1985, I was between flights at the Dallas-Fort Worth International Airport. I was in the American Airlines terminal, walking someplace with a couple of guys from the band, when I looked up and saw Debbie walking down the terminal in her American Airlines flight attendant's uniform. And, as usual, she was looking good.

Now, most of those girls who fly on the airlines won't look

around. They're either talking with other flight attendants or looking straight ahead thinking about where they need to be and when. But Debbie looked right at me. I punched one of the guys and said, "God Almighty, look at her!" We both kept walking our opposite directions, but we glanced at each other a time or two.

A little later I was on the phone to, of all people, Sherwood Cryer. I looked up and saw her passing by again, this time in the other direction, with the same flight attendants. It turns out their gate had been changed and they were walking back across the terminal to prepare for their flight at the new gate. I remember thinking how great she looked and how much I would like to talk with her. The gate was close by and they had a little time on their hands, so the flight attendants stayed right around the area. For some reason Debbie passed by again, to go into the gift shop or something. I decided not to tempt fate a third time. I dropped the phone, with Cryer still talking, walked up to her and said, "Look, I've just got to talk to you. I'm on the phone with my manager right now . . . but please, if you've got just a minute, I really want to talk to you."

She smiled and even turned a little red in the face and said, "Sure." I walked back over and picked up the phone that I had left dangling in the air. Cryer was still talking like nothing had happened, and I said, "Hey man, they're loadin' up the plane . . . I got to go right now."

I hung up the phone and we sat down and talked. I got her phone number, and then we left for our respective flights. A few days later I called her.

I told her I had a concert on June 12 at Billy Bob's Texas in Fort Worth, near where she lived, and asked her if she'd come meet me there. She said she would, and I felt like I was on top of the world.

You have to understand that Debbie is a very wonderful, beautiful, dynamic lady. I still feel like the luckiest man alive when I'm with her. If there ever was a Yellow Rose of Texas, this blonde lady was its inspiration.

Of course, Debbie is also very smart. So, being the smart lady she is, when June 12 and the concert at Billy Bob's came around, she didn't ride with a friend or let me send a car for her. She drove her own car — just in case things didn't work out. She seemed to have a pretty good time, enjoying the show and everyone out there.

She was a model as well as an attendant with the airline, which worked out pretty well for her. She could use her travel benefits to fly to places for modeling jobs, make herself available, and get the work without spending a lot of money. A lot of flight attendants use their benefits that way. It also came in handy while I was living out in California, because we could get together easier, whether in California, Texas, or someplace that I was performing.

Debbie met Cherish when Cherish was two years old, and they took to each other right away. In fact, she's been like a mother to my little girl. When Cherish came for a visit they would have the best time. And then when it was time to go back, Cherish would start crying, Debbie would be crying, and I'd be feeling terrible. We were a family, even way back then.

Debbie and I dated for about a year and a half, then got married. But the funny thing is I didn't ask her to marry me until she walked down the aisle at the ceremony. She had always told me she wouldn't marry me unless I asked her. I never did while we were dating, during the time we were making arrangements for the wedding, or during the trip to Maui where the ceremony was held. But I was afraid she might be serious about not marrying me if I didn't actually ask her. So, right before the preacher began to recite the "dearly beloveds," I turned to her and asked her if she would marry me. I don't know what the hell I would have done if she had said no.

Maui was the perfect place for the wedding. It is absolutely the most beautiful place on the earth. Every kind of flower you can imagine is there, and everything is so fresh and new. When Debbie walked toward me at the ceremony, Maui became the frame to the most beautiful picture I had ever seen. She was lovely.

My best man were Chris Coronado and a close friend I call Doctor Harry, an emergency room doctor in California. Doc had helped me cope with a lot of things in the previous few years — the divorce, my problems with Cryer, and so forth. He's still one of my best friends and probably always will be. When Debbie and I decided to get married, I knew Doc Harry would stand with me, because he had stood beside me all those years.

Debbie's matron of honor was Julie Crenshaw, wife of pro golfer Ben Crenshaw, another good friend of mine. Ben had been on the golf course that day and was running late. He got in such a hurry when he came running out of his hotel that he slipped and fell and got grass stains all over his white pants, which meant he had to go back in and change. That made him late to the wedding. At least he wasn't in front of thousands of people when it happened. I know how *that* feels.

One time I was playing at the Pasadena Rodeo. I had just bought a brand new suit that had been custom-made for Roy Clark. It turned out a little too snug for him, so I bought it. Apparently the fit was snug for me too.

The plan was for me to ride a horse out to the stage. I would gallop around the arena a few times as the band played a big introduction, wave at the crowds, then head up to the stage, jump off, grab a mike, and cut loose. Well, they brought that horse around for me to get on just outside the arena gate, and I swear that was the biggest, widest damn horse I had ever been on. Now, as most riders know, you're supposed to use your legs to sort of hold onto the animal and keep your balance, as well as keep your butt from getting busted on every gallop, while you gently guide him with the reins. Well, guiding wasn't the problem; he was a fine horse to ride. I just couldn't get my legs around that son of a bitch, much less get any leverage to hold on with. So, I got as comfortable as I could, heard the band hit the first chord to the opening number, gave the horse a little goose with my boot, and took off. I got about halfway around the damn arena, and suddenly I felt the rush of cool air right up my ass. That fat horse had made me rip my new pants, from the zipper all the way around my butt and clear up to my belt. I was showing my butt to 5,000 country music fans.

I wanted to just stay on the horse and sing once I got to the stage, but the microphone wouldn't reach. So, once the spotlight was off of me for a second, I got off the horse and jumped onto the stage. I did all of my numbers sort of hiding behind drums and amplifiers and such. They wanted me to

ride off the stage on that horse, but I said, "No, I don't think
so" and made them bring the tractor around to take me back
so no one could see my ripped-open pants.

Debbie thinks that is one of the funnier stories about me.
She has helped me learn to laugh at a lot of things in life,
things that aren't always that funny or that innocent.

We have been together for a few years now, and I really
can't imagine a life without Debbie. She helps keep me in line.
Sometimes, during my show, I like to joke about when I ask
her if everything were to fall apart — no more records, no
more concerts, nothing — would she still love me. When I say
that she looks at me and says "Of course I'll love you, Johnny.
I'll miss you — but I'll love you."

Seriously, though, we're partners and we face everything
together. We know it's much easier in this life when both pull
the wagon in the same direction. We also know that in depending on each other, the other one is there to provide the
support needed to endure times of difficulty. The hardest
thing we've both had to endure was the loss of our newborn
baby in March 1989.

Only five and a half months after Debbie became pregnant, our baby died at birth. We kept her in a room overnight
and slept with her. It was so hard to let her go with the man
from the funeral home the next morning. I had spent about
three or four hours alone with Heaven while Debbie was wak-
ing up. I baptized her and sat and held her. I really think it
helped us being able to spend time with our baby and having
the minister of the church come by and pray with us before
they took her away. It was better than never getting to see her
or hold her at all. There is no way to get over a loss like that.
You eventually have to learn to live with it.

Debbie and I want children, and we were naturally very
excited when she became pregnant with Heaven Lee. But
there was nothing anyone could do. She was simply too pre-
mature to survive.

Needless to say, it was tough on both of us. My Aunt
Mary Lou and Uncle Charles came out to be with us and help
us through. Without them I don't know what we would have

done. I know Debbie and I will never get over it. I've never had to do anything as hard as when I carried that little casket during the funeral. But we've had to move forward with our lives together.

One good thing that did come out of all that is that it put us a little closer to the Lord, and it brought Debbie and I closer together. I guess everything happens for a reason.

Some couples tend not to want to have a family after something like that happens, but Debbie and I know we want children. The doctors also have a good idea of what the problem was and how to guard against it in the future. Hopefully, before long we'll be able to start a family.

Debbie and I are partners. We work together with the marriage, the music, everything. She goes with me everywhere, and we both love it. At first, Mr. Macho here wanted to go everywhere by himself — just me and the guys, and all that. Debbie had different plans, and because of her caring devotion, she has really straightened my life up. Not a lot of partying. No whiskey drinking, just a beer every now and then. It's nothing Debbie demands of me; to the contrary, she doesn't make demands. I quit that stuff because I care for her and love her.

Sometimes I wonder why she has stayed with me. But when I ask her she says, "Because I love you, Johnny." I think if a person has someone like that beside him, he can do anything.

8: Roadwork and Play

The times out on the road were some of the most fun times I've ever had. It was what I had wanted to do all my life. Traveling across the country with the Urban Cowboy Band and Mickey Gilley was great.

Gilley tends to forget, but I was the one who came up with the name for the band. Right after the movie came out we were talking about the band's name. The group had been called the Bayou City Beats, which I couldn't stand. So, one day I said, "Mickey, why don't you just call them the Urban Cowboy Band?" He said, "I don't really know if I can do that." I said, "Sure you can . . . what the hell?" Well, he took my advice, and to this day the band is called the Urban Cowboy Band. It always made sense to me.

When we were out on the road we pulled all kinds of crap on each other. One night, I remember, I was all fired up. It was a big show, early in my career with Gilley, and I wanted everything to be perfect. When I was introduced I ran out on stage, plugged in my guitar, and started playing. All of a sudden my guitar just shorted out. Now, when you're on stage there are very few things as distracting as having a problem

126

like that. But all I could do was try to keep on going and hope the band's backup could help out. Well, I jerked the guitar around and hit a few chords and it came on again — then back off. So I messed with it some more while I kept singing, still hitting the chords to that first song. And it would do the same thing: come back on for a few seconds, then off. About that time the sound man came running out with a new amplifier chord, so I jerked out the one I had and threw it away, put in the new one, and plugged my guitar back into the amp. I played along some more and the same thing started happening again.

Well, by now the song was pretty well screwed, as was my great entrance, and in front of a big crowd at that. But I tried to maintain my cool while the sound man got another amplifier chord from another guitar player; still the same thing kept happening. We went through about three or four amplifier chords before I finally looked back and saw my drummer, Mike Schillaci, just cracking up. He couldn't stop laughing. Well, I might be slow on the uptake but it didn't take long for me to figure out I had been had — big time. As it turned out, he had replaced my guitar's electrical fuse with the blinker light fuse off of the turn signal in my car. So, the sound would just go on and off and on and off, with me just standing there trying to be cool. Everybody got a big kick out of it — the band, the audience, even me. A lot of times the crowd likes that kind of thing better than a slick open to a show.

Of course, I have to admit, I pulled my share of crap on people. Especially Gilley. In fact, Gilley thought that the incident with the blinker fuse was so damn funny that on another night I decided he should share in the fun. I got an aluminum bar and laid it across the strings of his piano before the show. Well, when the show started we introduced Gilley and he came running out and jumped right into his first song, running his hands up and down the keys like he does. But when he did, it sounded like a little toy piano. He had about the same reaction I had before; in fact, I think when he first hit the keys it was such a weird, out-of-place sound that it startled him. It got a hell of a laugh from everybody.

It didn't take long before I began to get more elaborate

with my tricks. On one occasion I contacted the animal
trainer for Clyde, the orangutan featured in a Clint Eastwood
movie. It was closing night at Harrah's main room in Reno,
and nothing had happened to Gilley all night. But while he
was talking with the audience between songs, getting them in
the mood for a serious ballad he was about to sing, I walked
out with Clyde. That brought a laugh because anyone who has
ever seen Clyde knows he is about the funniest looking ape in
the world. The trainer had taught me a few subtle hand sig-
nals to get Clyde to do certain things. So, when I walked out I
was talking with Clyde. I said, "Clyde, this is my friend
Mickey Gilley. Mickey, this is one of your biggest fans."
Mickey played it up right and said, "Well, hi, Clyde. How you
doin', man?" and joked with us a little. At this point, Gilley
knew something was up, because Clyde wasn't part of the
show and I usually pulled something on him on closing nights.

I treated Clyde like he was a real guest on the show. I
said, "Clyde, how do you like Mickey's singing?" and gave him
his cue just as I asked him. He started flapping those huge
ape lips of his and shaking his head no. I said, "Now, come on,
Clyde, Mickey's my friend and I think he sings a pretty song.
What do you really think about his singing?" I cued him and
he turned to Gilley, smiled, and flipped him the bird with a
finger that must be a foot long if it's an inch. Everybody
started laughing. Even Gilley was laughing so hard he
couldn't stand up. Of course, I acted like I was getting on to
him, then I turned around and said, "Well, Clyde, what about
this great Urban Cowboy Band?" He shot the band the bird.
Now the audience was rolling. I asked Clyde about Harrah's
wonderful orchestra, and right on cue he flipped the orchestra
the bird. "Well, Clyde, surely you think the audience is nice
. . . all these fine folks out here to see us?" The ape spread that
ugly-faced, stupid smile of his at the audience . . . and flipped
them off too. They laughed more and Gilley completely lost
his composure.

It took Gilley a while to get back into the mood for that
serious ballad. In fact, he kept laughing every time he
thought about that damn ape. For a minute I didn't think he
was going to be able to sing the song. But that incident turned

out to be mild compared to what I did to him sometime later.

It was another closing night at Harrah's, my night to strike. (Kind of like the werewolf that prowls on the night of a full moon.) I went out and hired a female impersonator. I knew Gilley always sang, "The Girls All Get Prettier At Closing Time" just before he ended the show, and I knew that on that particular night the end of the show was going to bring the house down with it.

He did the whole show and nothing happened, though I know he kept looking over his shoulder for my practical joke to pop up. Everything went along like clockwork. Then, as soon as he started singing "The Girls All Get Prettier At Closing Time," this 300-pound guy, dressed in a red sequin party dress, came out dancing behind him. Well, the audience just went nuts, and of course Gilley thought he was just tearing them up. His hands were flying way up high off that piano like his cousin Jerry Lee Lewis. Of course, he couldn't see the guy behind him, dancing like an idiot. Gilley really got into the song, and the dancer really started shaking it. Gilley was just burning those keys like there was no tomorrow.

The room finally got so wild that he looked behind him and saw this fat "woman" bumping and grinding. Well, Gilley tried to act cool and make like this was part of the show, so he got up and started dancing with what he thought was a woman. Pretty soon the female impersonator picked him up and slung him all over the stage, and the crowd was going crazy. Right about then, the dancer gave Gilley a big 'ol kiss on the forehead — and left a pair of six-inch lipstick marks you could see in the dark. On the next twirl, the impersonator gave Gilley another big kiss on the cheek. Before it was over, Gilley had lipstick all over his face, and the crowd was loving it.

Gilley made it back over to the piano and finished out this hot number with a big old rip right across the piano keys, then jumped up, grabbed what he thought was just a fat, ugly woman, and kissed that dude square on the mouth. As soon as he did, the dude stepped back and pulled off his wig. The whole place fell out. Gilley just stood there with his mouth hanging open — he couldn't even move.

The funny thing was, after a while, if I didn't pull anything on Mickey, especially on closing night, he would almost
go crazy waiting for something to happen. But it was rare for
me not to try some kind of joke on him. Sometimes I wouldn't
get quite so "show stopping" with it; I'd just "fix" things for
him. Like when he would start to leave the piano to sing a few
songs, he might reach over to grab a microphone lying on a
towel and pull up a mike with an apple stuck on top instead of
a mike screen. But usually, if I went to the trouble of pulling
a joke on him, I'd make sure it was good, because, as they say
in the commercial, I knew he was worth it.

Once, while we were in Reno at Harrah's, Gilley had decided not to come down early and watch my show. I would
open the show, then introduce him and he'd do his thing, so a
lot of times he'd watch my show before he went on. Well, on
this night he was still upstairs when I was on. He had seen the
act hundreds of times, I guess, so he knew how to judge the
time left before he went on by what I was doing. "Lookin' For
Love" was what I would end my portion of the show with before introducing Gilley, which meant he had to be right there
in the wings, waiting, so he could come on right after. As I
said, he knew my show so well, he just listened to the speakers
in his dressing room to see where I was and would know at
any given minute how long he had. However, on this particular night, I had one of the technicians make a tape of the show
that we had done the night before so it would play in Gilley's
dressing room. When Gilley heard it, he would think he was
hearing the show that evening "live."

There he was, walking around in his dressing room and
acting cool, like he had just won a million dollars in the ca-
sino, when he turned up the sound and heard "Lookin' For
Love" (we had run the tape ahead to the end of my show). He
jumped into his show clothes and hauled ass down to the main
room at Harrah's and damn near out onto the stage before
somebody caught him — and there I was, about halfway
through my show. He told me later that that was the quickest
he had ever gotten dressed without the sound of a husband
coming home early.

Sometimes our "incidents" didn't happen on stage. We were in Detroit, at the height of the popularity of the *Urban Cowboy* movie, as the guests of radio station WWWW. I was elated that our music was being heard all over the country. I thought it was the greatest thing since M&M's. When we got to Detroit, they picked us up in a helicopter at the airport and took us to an Urban Cowboy type of saloon. I did a demonstration on their mechanical bull, we played a little, and then signed autographs all night long. The people were great, and we were having a hell of a time. Later on that night we went out on the town and partied our butts off in first-class style.

We had been teamed up with some big-time radio disc jockeys and were riding in a limousine with them and some ladies they knew. I had on the same cowboy hat that had become my trademark and that I had worn on all of my album covers. It was the one with the javelina tusks and the agate stone. I never parted with it; it was special to me. Besides that, it was a good-looking and very well-made hat, not to mention expensive — as good cowboy hats are.

Well, one of the girls riding in the car wanted to see my hat. Now, a lot of people like to look at cowboy hats, especially in that part of the country where they aren't as common as they are in Texas. Of course, we had been out dancing, drinking, and raising hell all night and I just thought she wanted to see my damn hat. So I handed it to her and didn't pay much attention until I heard all of this coughing and gagging. I looked back, and the bitch was throwing up . . . *in my hat!*

I yelled at the driver to pull over, grabbed my hat, and opened the door. It was raining like a son of a bitch that night. There I was, hanging out of a limousine, dumping vomit out of my hat, slinging it up against the car and getting splashed by passing cars and trucks in the rain. I couldn't believe that bitch had vomited in my hat, and I had a gig the next day where I needed to wear it.

I got back to the hotel and washed my hat out in the bathtub, and tried as best I could to reshape it myself. There just ain't cowboy hat shops on every street corner in Detroit. About all I could do was set it on the air conditioner vent in the hotel room and hope that it dried out and that there wouldn't be any of that stringy stuff left in there. Naturally, it shrunk a little, and as soon as I got back to Texas I tried to get it professionally shaped, but as hat owners know they just ain't the same after they've been soaked — especially when someone has puked in them.

I still can't believe that someone threw up in my best god-damn cowboy hat.

Perhaps the funniest thing I ever saw, besides Gilley's face when he realized he had kissed a man, was when Herve Villechaize (the little guy from "Fantasy Island") came to see us after a show one night in Las Vegas. I had just shot an epi-sode of "Fantasy Island" and was back on the road. Herve caught the show and came backstage to my dressing room to say hello. I remember he came in with two big bodyguards who stood about six feet tall, and I'll give Vegas odds that they had to weigh 350 pounds each. Now, obviously he had these guys around for his protection, and they were doing a good job, standing on either side of him. But apparently they weren't doing a perfect job. Despite all of their protection, my drum-mer walked in just as Herve turned to leave and the doorknob caught Herve square in the head and knocked the ever living crap right out of him.

I know it was painful, but I swear I have never seen a fun-nier sight. He ran all over the room rubbing his little bitty old head and yelling, "Aw, sheet . . . aw, got-dameet . . . aw, sheet." He looked like a little jack-in-the-box running around the room holding his head. Fortunately, it wasn't serious. But after that I never could see him on TV when he would point and say, "Da plane . . . da plane!" without remembering that night.

About the second funniest thing I ever saw offstage was one night at the Palomino Club in North Hollywood. At the time there was no condom machine in the men's room of the Palomino, but believe it or not, there was a damn cologne ma-chine in there. Only in North Hollywood would you find a co-logne machine in the men's room. It seemed rather strange to me. Most guys in North Hollywood are probably particular about what color underwear they put on, so why would they want some generic cologne out of a machine? The way it worked, you put two quarters in and the machine sprayed you with a light mist.

Well, one night, after a show, I was in the men's room there, minding my own business at the urinal, when this little Japanese guy came in. He did whatever he came in to do, went over to the sink and washed his hands. Then he looked at the machine with a big smile. To me he said, "Ca-rone?" Hell, I didn't know what he was trying to say. He just kept pointing at his crotch then at the machine and saying, "Ca-rone, ca-rone?" or something like that. I just smiled back and shook my head and said, "Yeah, yeah." I had no idea what he was trying to say until he put two quarters in. About the time I figured out that he thought it was a condom machine and tried to warn him, he bent down about eye level with the dispenser and got his eyes and nose full of cologne. He coughed and spat and cussed Japanese and rolled all over those walls. I mean, he was some kind of pissed. Not only that, he still didn't have a condom.

Before I laugh too hard about that guy, I'd better tell another one on me. Once I bought a hairpiece. Joe Ladd over at KIKK Radio talked me into it. He and I were slowly watching each other's hair thin out over time, and he finally got himself a hairpiece. Now, this wasn't no ordinary rug; this was an expertly constructed hairpiece that looked so real a woman running her hands through it couldn't tell the difference. Well, Joe talked me into getting one. So, I saved up what money I was getting from Cryer at the time and put down about five hundred dollars on the most perfect hairpiece I had ever seen in my life. They took a sample of my hair and came back a few days later with a toupee that looked like it came off my scalp.

I was instructed how to attach it properly so it wouldn't come off. And Joe added his two cents worth of instructions, having experienced the life of a toupee wearer. I remember one thing he told me was to be careful in bars that had those eight- or ten-foot square fans blowing sideways across the dance floor, because if I walked in front of them the wrong way it would blow my hairpiece up.

Well, one night I had a date with a girl all the way across Houston from Gilley's. Gilley and I drove over after the show to meet her and some of her friends for a party. Now, I didn't want to be embarrassed if my hairpiece came off, so I took it off and put it in the glove compartment. I figured she and I had probably had enough to drink by that time of the night and that she wouldn't be able to tell if I had a hairpiece on or not. But I remembered another warning Joe gave me about the toupee: "Don't put it in the glove compartment of your car, because you might be riding around with some girl, and she might open that glove box to do whatever and she'll find your hairpiece. Then you really will be embarrassed." So I took his advice and I put the hairpiece under the seat of the car, thinking no one would ever find it there.

The next day was a beautiful Sunday and I was driving back. I had a fine-looking Lincoln Continental at the time and took great care of that car. I didn't like for it to have a speck of dust on it (which can be impossible in the Houston area), so I decided to stop at this service station I used in Pasadena on Southmore Street and have the fellows there clean it up. When I pulled up I told them, "Fill it up, wash and wax it." I had no more than gotten out of the car when what seemed like four thousand men with rags and vacuum cleaners hit that car and were going to town. All of a sudden I heard one of the vacuum hoses sort of gag and cough, and I realized I had left my goddamn five-hundred-dollar hairpiece under the seat. Too late now, Jack, it was gone. I was too embarrassed to say anything about it, but I decided then and there that I had lost my hair twice now, so to hell with it. I wasn't going to try and replace it anymore.

I guess I'm lucky it was my hair and not my eye that I lost, like my guitar player did — in a poker game.

Mike Shillaci was always doing something off the wall, like screwing with the fuse in my guitar. Well, one night, while we were on the bus, we all got up a poker game. It was something we did all the time to make the trip between gigs go by faster. Gilley used to hate for us to gamble because some of the guys would lose all their money and then ask Gilley for more. Well, that happened to Little Henry one night. He got into a bet and ran out of money and didn't want to ask Gilley for more, so he bet the only thing he had left — his glass eye.

We had been drinking beer after the show that night, and were all pretty tight, so what the hell? The man wanted to wager his glass eye, so we let him wager his glass eye. Well, lady luck frowned on the one-eyed picker and Mike won Little Henry's damn eye. Of course, Henry was just a little pissed off that he had been stupid enough to bet his eye and lose, and Mike had been enough of a butt to take it. So, while we all sat up in the front of the bus getting grossed out by Henry without an eye, Mike slipped back to the rear of the bus. A few minutes later Mike came out and he had Henry's eye stuck in his rear, saying, "I see you, Henry." Henry jumped up madder than a hornet. I thought he was going to whip Mike's butt right there, one-eyed and all. Mike finally gave him his eye back.

When we traveled, everybody was subject to our bullshit, especially mine. Sometimes I'd "help" our bus driver, Joe, when he was taking us all somewhere. He prided himself on knowing where he was at all times, and wouldn't admit to being lost if his life depended on it. I've got to say, we saw a lot of scenic America that most people going that same way don't get to see, you understand. But according to Joe, we were never lost.

Of course, a few times I was partially to blame for the scenic routes. I'd get in the back of the bus with a CB walkie-talkie I had at the time and call him like I was another truck driver somewhere along the road. I'd talk with him awhile and eventually he would ask directions. I'd give him directions when I didn't even know where we were, and have him so screwed up that one time he took us fifty miles out of the way. After offering directions with that trucker lingo, I'd go up front and casually ask him if he knew where we were. He'd say, "Oh yeah, boss, I know right where we're at. Everything's fine." Then I'd go back and give him some more helpful advice.

Once I even pissed him off. I told him I was a trucker who had passed him and said I thought he was about the ugliest son of a bitch there was. Well, hell, he was ready to stop the bus and whip that trucker's ass right there. As it turned out, we told him what happened and caught his ass lying about being lost, and he never lived that down.

Sometimes when we got bored traveling from place to place we would draw on people in the band while they slept. It was especially easy when we were flying in the airplane Gilley and I owned. We'd cut the oxygen down a little and make everybody who had had a little bit to drink go to sleep, then we'd draw on them. One time Mike Schillaci passed out and I drew big 'ol spiders all over his face. Now, Mike thought he was the funniest bastard that ever lived, especially after the blinking fuse episode. So after he woke up and the plane landed, he went walking through the airport in St. Louis. Everybody was pointing and laughing at him, and he thought it was because of the stupid little things he was saying as he walked through. Well, he made it to the bar and people started cracking up every time he said something. Now he thought he was the newest undiscovered stand-up comic. Well, at one point he yelled at the bartender to get his ass over there and get him a drink. The bartender told him that he didn't have to pay any attention to somebody with bugs all over his head. Mike leaned over and looked into a decorative mirror on the wall and just freaked out.

But that wasn't it for Mr. Schillaci, because I kept remembering the amplifier chord incident. Again, while we were flying back from somewhere, he fell asleep and I sneaked over and painted one of his cheeks blue. I noticed it didn't wake him so I colored his other cheek red. Well, he still didn't wake up so I thought, "Hell, this is a free ride." I proceeded to paint his forehead black and his chin red and blue and black. He was so painted up he looked like an aborigine tribesman. When we landed, he woke up and got off the plane and headed for the loving arms of his wife — and damn near scared the hell out of her right there in the airport.

On another occasion, our guitar picker went into a convenience store to get something. While he was asleep on the bus I had painted one of his fingernails red. He came out and looked at me and said, "You son of a bitch, I didn't know you had painted my fingernail red and that lady inside was laughing at me." What he didn't realize was that I had also painted a big ol' red bug right on his forehead.

The guys probably didn't pull as much stuff on me as I pulled on them, because I could do myself in pretty well without their help. I remember one night when I was supposed to sing for the La Porte Police Department. Sometime before I had sat in with a band the police department had. A friend of mine, Ben Greene, who was a cop on the force, had introduced me to them. After we jammed a while they asked me to come back and sing at their police department party. I told them I'd be happy to. Then I made arrangements so that I could do my thing at Gilley's, leave the club, drive to La Porte and do their party, and still be back in time for my next show at Gilley's.

I remember that night I had on a black rhinestone outfit that looked like something Elvis might have worn. I felt great and was looking sharp. I wanted to put on a good show for these guys because they do important work and I had gotten to know them. Well, as soon as I finished my first show at Gilley's, I jumped into the car and headed for La Porte, just up the road a ways.

I finally arrived at the La Porte Civic Center parking lot and noticed quite a few Hispanics hanging around the parking lot and pouring out of the door to the big party going on inside. I thought, "Man, there's sure a lot of Mexicans on the La Porte police force." Well, I walked on into a jam-packed civic center with my guitar case in hand and everybody was looking at me. I figured it was the jet black outfit. I walked on up to the bandstand and noticed it was a mariachi band playing some kick-ass Latino music and I thought, "Hell, it must be a Mexican theme for the party." I looked around for somebody I recognized, when about that time a fellow walked up and said, "Señor, can I help you?"

I said "Yeah, I'm looking for Ben Greene."

"Who?"

"Ben Greene . . . of the La Porte Police Department."

Well, the old guy kind of chuckled and then I found out the police department party had been held the previous night. I had gotten my nights mixed up! As it turned out, I had

walked in on a Mexican wedding party. At least I came for-
mal.

On my good friend Doc Harry's birthday one year, I was
supposed to be at his party in California. I thought I was off
that night, but Cryer slipped a job on me when someone can-
celed at Billy Bob's. He told me that the job had been scheduled for months. I knew he was lying to me. So that night I
asked the club owner to pay me in cash, and I took it all to
lease a Lear jet to fly me to California from Dallas. A limo
waited for me at the end of the runway so I could make it to
the party before it was over and give Doc Harry the cowboy
boots I had bought him. He always wore boots to work at the
hospital. Cryer hit the ceiling when he found out he wasn't
going to get the money I made that night. He asked me if I had
lost my mind. I didn't give a damn because I had a ball doing
what I did!

After all of the pranks and stunts I've pulled on people
over the years, there is now someone who is destined to put
me in my place: Cherish. We once took her to a baseball game
in Atlanta to watch Rick Sutcliffe and Jody Davis, two good
friends of ours, play ball. What a beautiful town and tremendous baseball park. Debbie, Cherish (who was about four at
the time), and I were there with Jody and Rick's wives and
just having a great time.

Now, all her life, I've jokingly called Cherish "peckerhead." In fact, that's what she calls me sometimes. We'll get to
playing around with each other and laughing and I'll say,
"You little peckerhead," and she'll copy me and laugh and say,
"You little peckerhead!" Obviously, she had no idea how that
sounded; it was just fun to us. Of course, every parent knows
how that kind of fun can backfire sometimes into a very embarrassing situation.

Well, we're at this ballgame in Atlanta, and down a few
rows in front of us was this Little League team. Their coach
must have brought them to the game, and those little guys
were having the time of their lives. Pretty soon Jody hit a
home run and the place went wild, everybody hollering and

screaming. Then, just as the crowd noise subsided, Cherish stood up to yell at her baseball buddy Jody. She cupped her little hands around her mouth and screamed at the top of her lungs: "Way to go, you little peckerhead!" That whole Little League team turned around and just rolled, including the coach. They acted like it was the funniest thing they had ever heard. Cherish was just as serious as she could be about applauding her big buddy. Of course, it embarrassed the hell out of Debbie, but it was funny.

Cherish struck again when she and Debbie and I were on a cruise ship one time. During that trip, Cherish got mad at me because I forgot to call her up to sing with me while I sang "Lookin' For Love," which I usually did. She didn't speak to me for quite a while after that, but she finally forgot about it when something better came along to take her mind off things. Then one day we were sunning out near the fantail of the ship when Cherish wandered over to a set of drums left by a small combo group that would perform there at night. She yelled at me, "Hey, Dad!" Well, I didn't pay any attention to her. Finally, she started beating on the drums, yelling, "Hey, Dad!" So, I thought I'd fool with her and not pay attention, and that would get the best of her. Bad thinking. After yelling at me several times and getting no response, she reached over and figured out how to turn the microphone on. The next thing I hear, bellowing out of the speakers across the ship's deck, which is full of people, is, "Hey, you peckerhead!" Of course, everybody cracked up. I jumped up and looked around, and there was sweet little innocent Cherish on those drums, grinning from ear to ear.

9: Drinkin', Drugs, and Disaster

One of the hazards of the music industry, no doubt, is the prevalence of illicit drugs. Many entertainers, just like many athletes — and for that matter, doctors, lawyers, and home-makers — use drugs. I would say the most widespread abuse is through alcohol. Most people don't think of alcohol as a drug. I know I usually don't, but it is a drug and it can affect your life. My $14,000 paternity suit, by a girl I had never touched, was due in part to the fact I signed my autograph for her while I was drunk and didn't have my wits about me to see what was going on. But, like most people, I never thought of alcohol as a drug, because we weren't raised to think of it in that manner. The first thing that comes to my mind when someone says drugs is something like cocaine or speed.

The truth of the matter is, I had never used hard drugs before I got in the business. I knew when I was growing up there was a thing called dope. I didn't know what dope looked like. I thought maybe it looked like toothpaste or something. I really just had no idea what it was. That changed when I became an adult, and especially when I started singing for a living.

One night, while Gilley was separated from his wife, I

asked him for a diet pill. I knew he had taken a few before, but I had no idea what speed was or uppers or downers or anything. I just needed something to pick me up and help me make it through the show. I said, "Gilley, give me a diet pill." So, Gilley, who was coping with personal and professional pressures of his own, threw three pills on the bed in the hotel room as we stood there talking. I had never really even looked at the pills before, and only called them "diet" pills because that's what everyone else called them. I looked at the pills after Gilley left and thought that was what I was supposed to take — all of them. When I was a kid, my mom or aunt would give me one aspirin when I got sick, and as I got a little older I noticed they would give me two. I just figured that whatever was given to me was the correct dosage.

Now, with the exception of beer, my body, to that point, had been as pure as a bar of Ivory Soap. I picked up the pills and thought, "Well, I ought not take all three of these. I don't need them . . . I'll just take two." Two, mind you! That's enough to make a horse go crazy. All I remember was that one was black and the other was yellow. Now, it took a while for them to really kick in, but when we went to work that night I couldn't stop singing, dancing, or picking. Whatever I could do or get away with on the stage I did. I wouldn't even let Gilley on the stage. I wanted to stay up there doing songs and playing music.

I remember Gilley got pissed off, but hell, I was a busy son of a bitch that night. I was doing the best damn job I had done in years. In reality it probably wasn't the best, but it sure as hell was the most I had done in one show. The crowd really got their money's worth from me that night.

I couldn't quit singing. I couldn't quit talking. I was wound tighter than a clock. After we got through working, I asked a friend of mine if he wanted some coffee. We usually went somewhere there in Pasadena or maybe into Houston. Hell, I got in the car and drove to San Antonio — for coffee.

So that was my first experience with drugs. Unfortunately, I didn't learn my lesson that first time. But now neither Gilley nor I do that stuff anymore because we don't need it, and it will damn sure kill you.

One night our bass player, Captain Sid we used to call him, was going to slip me something at the bar . . . a little "pick me up." I walked up to him and said, "Goddamn, man, I'm just so tired . . . you got anything I could take, brother?" He said, "Yeah, I'll get you something when we take a break." So I went back and finished another set on the bandstand, just begging for it to end so I could get over and let Sid give me something to finish the night with.

Well, something made me sense that it just wasn't right, because when the break came and we walked over to the bar, the whole band was gathered around behind him. He went ahead and slid me something underneath the bar. We had to be real covert about it, because the last thing I needed was to get busted in a bar, especially the bar where I worked.

I kept looking around like nothing was going on while Sid dropped something in my hand. I didn't want to look at it for fear someone, like an undercover cop, would see me and catch on to what was going on.

I felt it and it seemed kind of mushy, and I thought, "What the hell is this?" As I continued to feel of it in my hand, I became more and more puzzled about what it was. Finally, my paranoia about being caught fell by the wayside, just enough to casually ease it out from under the bar and start to blindly swallow it. That's when I saw some of my band members giggling. Thank God, I looked down before I put it in my mouth. Sid had been treating a wart on his hand with some medicine, and it had finally come off. And Sid had slipped me that damn wart! I almost threw up just thinking about what might have been. I looked at him, as he was laughing his ass off, and said, "One day I will pay you back."

Many months went by and one night a guy was out at the club and gave me some kind of a painkiller or downer. As fate would have it, Sid came to me saying, "Man, you got anything that can get me up?" I said, "I sure do, buddy, but there's one thing about this . . . you got to drink a shot of whiskey with it to kick it right in." Sid didn't even bat an eye. He got a shot of whiskey and looked at the pill, only long enough to comment on the fact it looked pretty big, then took it.

By the time we got back up on stage, the drug had taken effect. I was trying to sing and his bass playing got slower and slower and slower. By the time Gilley got up there, Sid couldn't even play and could barely stand up. Gilley chewed him out. Sid told Gilley in slurred and slow speech, "I know . . . what to . . . do . . . But I . . . just . . . can't get my . . . hands . . . there . . . in time . . . to do it."

Gilley kicked his ass off stage and we had to get the fiddle player to play bass. Sid got so freaked out over the whole thing he asked me how long it would last. I said, "You remember that wart you gave me?" He said, "Aw shit." I just said, "This dude's going to last three days." Of course it didn't, but he stayed worried for the rest of the night.

Taking drugs was something I did when I was young and dumb. I thought it was the cool thing to do, or that maybe it was just what you did in the music business.

I remember the first time I got to work a concert with the Charlie Daniels Band. I walked into the big room they had backstage and saw all these hypodermic needles lined up on a table draped with a white linen tablecloth. I thought, "Well, this must be what you do." What I didn't know, and soon found out, was that there were nurses there administering vitamin B-12 with those syringes. Charlie doesn't use drugs, nor does anyone in his band. But he keeps trained professionals around to provide vitamin B-12 for his people. When you travel a lot, your resistance tends to get low and you become susceptible to colds and the flu. This was what Charlie did to help keep his folks healthy on those grueling road tours.

Fortunately, I learned what drugs and drug abuse were all about before it was too late. A lot of people don't. Maybe you can't expect someone to realize what's going to happen to them. I know I was stubborn enough not to hear a word anyone said.

Reflection:
Through the Eyes of Bubba

One of Johnny's best friends is Bubba Rigby. Bubba works for the city of La Porte, near Houston, as a purchasing agent. The two have known each other for about twenty years, ever since Johnny's days at the Nesadale Club in Dickinson. Bubba is a rather quiet man, someone who listens when a friend needs to talk, and he knows Johnny fairly well.

"He's a hard person to get to know," Bubba says, "but once you get to know him, you couldn't ask for a nicer person. We tend to stay out of each other's personal business unless asked, and I think that's why we've gotten along so well all these years. Johnny is a private man when he's not performing, and I respect that."

Having known Johnny for so long, Bubba has seen him in almost every kind of situation. He knows what gets to Johnny, and what he just lets roll off his back.

"Johnny used to be a fairly moody person, but he's mellowed a lot. I know Debbie has had a lot to do with that. She's good for him. I've known her since they began dating, and she's a very nice lady.

"I met his former wife, Charlene Tilton, back in the early eighties . . . I remember it was during a road trip. Johnny took

me along during a tour with Mickey Gilley through much of the
South and Southwest as a products salesman, selling hats and
belt buckles and things at the concerts. The first place he played
on that particular trip was Los Angeles, and that's when I met
Charlene. She was nice to look at, I'll have to admit, but she was
strange, sort of hard to figure out. She would look at you and say
one thing and mean something entirely different. I don't believe
I had ever met a person quite as out of the ordinary as Charlene
Tilton. I really am not sure why Johnny and Charlene got married, except maybe he found her behavior interesting. I think it
seemed like to Johnny to be the logical thing to do. Here they
were dating, they were both stars, and when they found out
Cherish was on the way, I guess it just seemed to them to be the
next step."

Bubba was one of the people Johnny could trust, and when
he and Tilton divorced, if Johnny talked about it much it was to
Bubba. Still, as Bubba tells it, Johnny seemed to keep everything to himself, not even sharing his feelings with his best
friend, except on rare occasions.

"When they divorced I know it was traumatic for him, as
any divorce could be for anyone. Sometimes he would call and we
would talk, and I could tell, even if we did talk about the divorce
or Charlene, it just made him feel better to talk. There really
wasn't much I could do. I mean, what do you tell a man that will
make him feel better after his wife has taken the baby and left
him? All I could do most of the time was listen. So, I know it affected him and his performances. But things usually do affect a
performer's work.

"I remember once when he and Gilley had a falling out over
some things, and Gilley didn't take him on the road for a few
weeks. He was performing at the club. That night, every song he
sang was a tear-jerking, beer-drinking song, and that's just not
Johnny's style. He's upbeat and has a great time on stage and in-
teracts with the audience very well . . . Some say a country
singer is at his best when things get him down. If that's true,
Johnny was soaring after Charlene left him. The ironic part of it
is, I know the fact that Cherish was gone affected him more than
the fact Charlene had left."

Bubba had a firsthand look at things during the filming of

Urban Cowboy on location at Gilley's. He remembers it as almost a three-ring circus.

"It had its good points and its bad points. I used to watch the
people that they used inside the club as extras. They were always excited about being in the movie, but they used to complain
about being treated like cattle — being herded from one place to
another so they could hurry up and do this or that . . . or more
often than not, just wait."

The production of a major motion picture is impressive in
many ways, intimidating in others, and downright boring for the
most part. Bubba saw that Larry Gatlin and the Gatlin Brothers
were right when they sang "all that glitters is not gold." In this
case, all that glittered, namely the idea of being a star in a
movie, paled in its glamour.

"All in all, it was very interesting to watch the filming then
see the finished product. I had never seen a motion picture being
shot before, and the thing that stands out most in my mind was
the number of times they would shoot a scene just to get a few
seconds of the movie produced . . . As far as the content of the
movie, I have to say it was a pretty fair representation of the
people in that area, and the people who went to Gilley's a lot. I
never got a chance to meet John Travolta or Debra Winger, but I
think they did a pretty good job in the movie of making their
characters convincing.

"I remember when I found out Johnny was singing the biggest song in the movie, which turned out to be the biggest hit of
his career, 'Lookin' For Love,' I was pretty excited for him. It was
the break he had worked hard for all his life. I thought it was
pretty funny when I found out he had picked the song out of a
cardboard box full of other songs, kind of like pulling a name out
of a hat for a door prize at a party. He could have just as easily
pulled the wrong tape and ended up with a dead-end song."

One of the times Bubba remembers as perhaps the most
moving when he was around Johnny was the night singing legend Rick Nelson was killed — New Year's Eve, 1986. Rick Nelson was one of Johnny's idols. The country singer from Alta
Loma, Texas, who had gone to the top of the world with numer-
ous hits and gold records and albums, was a lifelong fan of Rick
Nelson's. Right beside his multimillion-copy hits, Johnny had
every record and album his idol ever recorded. Johnny and Rick

had played together before, something Johnny had dreamed of
all his life. On this particular night, New Year's Eve, they were
to play in Dallas just down the street from each other at two different New Year's parties.

Johnny was on the phone with his manager at the time,
when most of the others there, including his soon-to-be wife,
Debbie, had just heard the news of Rick's plane going down in far
East Texas as the singer and his band traveled to Dallas that
night. At first, no one wanted to tell Johnny, because it was just
before he was to go on and give his own concert for the Dallas Police Association. But just as Johnny was about to hang up the
phone, his manager broke the news to him. Johnny was devastated.

After the show for the police officers, Johnny and his whole
band went to the Park Suites, where Rick was to have played,
and performed a concert of Rick Nelson hits for an appreciative
but mournful crowd. Then Johnny just walked outside alone and
looked up at the stars.

"I walked out and put my hand on his shoulder," Bubba recalls. "I said, 'You all right?' He said, 'Yeah,' and I knew it was
one of those times when he wanted to be alone, so I left him
there. He stood out there looking at the stars for a very long
time."

When recalling that cold night, Johnny says he doesn't remember how long he stared up into the night sky. He just remembers looking up at the stars, thinking about Rick, Otis Red-
ding, and Buddy Holly. And he remembers crying.

After Johnny played at the Park Suites, he and the band
went out to eat, as they usually do after a show. Most of the time
the singer has a ferocious appetite, and will eat anything from
ham and eggs to pizza and barbecue, no matter what time of the
morning it is when the show is over. But on this particular night,
Johnny just went along at the urging of Debbie. Bubba remembers they found a pancake place and went inside.

"Johnny was still down," Bubba thinks back. "We were
trying to cheer him up as best as we could, all the guys and Debbie. Then all of a sudden this fellow comes over to the table. He
was a black guy, wearing just some old jogging shorts and a pullover shirt . . . and here it was freezing outside. He said, 'Aren't
you Johnny Lee?' Johnny said, 'Yes, I am.' Well, the fellow

smiled and said, 'Hey man, you need a singer?' Johnny kind of
smiled and said, 'Well, man, can you sing?' So the guy runs over
to the jukebox and drops in a quarter on a Lionel Ritchie tune
and begins to audition right there in the restaurant. And what's
more, he was terrible. He couldn't carry a tune in a bucket.
Johnny started laughing and everybody in the restaurant
started laughing. Then when it was over, the guy says, 'What'd
you think?' Johnny said, 'Well, friend, I think it needs a little
more work.' So the guy runs back to the jukebox and drops another quarter and starts all over again. We laughed our butts off
that night.

"Once he had an offer from a real musician, a saxophone
player, who said he would work for $35 a week and would even
sleep on the bus so Johnny wouldn't have to pay for a hotel room
for him. That was down at a little dive outside of Houston called
the Four Palms. It had a fairly sleazy reputation, though we
went there from time to time to get away from everything. The
rumor was the shift workers' wives did their shifts there. When
their husbands left for the two o'clock shift, they would leave for
the Four Palms. When the shifts changed at the plants, the
wives changed shifts at the Four Palms."

Johnny is renowned for playing jokes on people. Bubba recalls a typical routine. "One night we were out eating after a
show and a couple of women, a mother and her daughter, kept
watching us from one of the tables. Finally, they both came over
and introduced themselves to Johnny and told him how much
they enjoyed his work. He thanked them and then turned to me
and said, 'And of course, you ladies know Bubba Rigby.' Well,
naturally they didn't and looked puzzled when he introduced me.
Then he said, 'I can't believe you know me and you don't know
Bubba. I thought every country music fan in the world knew
Bubba.' Well, they smiled politely at me, looked at Johnny,
glanced at each other, and nervously smiled back at me again
. . . They went back to their table and kept looking back at me,
trying to figure out what hit I had recorded, I guess.

"He used to do that in shows — introduce one or two of us
who happened to be in the audience, but without telling the audience what we were supposed to be famous for, just to see what
would happen. He did it once with his sound man Bert Frilout.
He stopped right in the middle of the song he was singing as Bert

walked into the place and said, 'Ladies and gentlemen, I'd like
for you to meet the one and only, Mr. Bert Frilout. It's a pleasure
you could be with us tonight, Bert.' Well, the spotlights came
around and hit Bert, he waved and everybody cheered. They
didn't have a clue who they were applauding. A second or two
later, here comes some little guy with a camera, stumbling over
people, crossing over seats, about to kill himself . . . just to get a
picture of Bert."

"Me and Mickey and the Brokaw boys!"

With Roger Miller at ACMA Awards, 1982.

John Boyland produced "Lookin' For Love" and "Cherokee Fiddle."

Johnny and Conway Twitty.

Johnny with Charley and Rosene
Pride, 1982.

Doug Kershaw, Johnny and Roger Miller, 1982.

Joining Doug Kershaw at Tucson Open, 1986.

Tony Orlando, Johnny's mom at Lake Tahoe, 1982.

"My award — Most Promising Male Vocalist." Johnny and Bill Boyd at ACMA Awards, 1981.

The "Yellow Rose of Texas," Lane Brody and Johnny Lee, 1987.

Johnny and Marvin Gaye, 1983.

Chubby Checker

Ace Cannon at Johnny Lee golf
tournament, 1986.

Mickey Gilley, Johnny, and Dottie
West, 1982.

Johnny and Scatman Crothers

With Coach Darrell Royal.

Billy Martin at the Stockyards in Nashville, 1986.

B. B. King

Rudy Gatlin.

Johnny Rodriguez, 1983.

Singing with Michael Martin Murphy.

James Brown

Lacy J. Dalton

Johnny and Bob Hope.

Billy Boyd, Mr. and Mrs. Dick Clark, and Johnny, 1981.

With Charlie Daniels.

Johnny, John Denver, and Mickey Gilley.

"Don't Rita Coolidge look good in
my hat?"

Willie Nelson

Johnny was adopted into the Kiowa tribe. Kiowa chief at left and Indian
brother, Ray Darby, at right.

With Alan Shepard.

Lawrence Taylor and Johnny. "He told me to teach him how to sing, and he would teach me how to hit. I said I already knew how to hit."

Alan Hale of "Gilligan's Island," Debbie, and Johnny at Doug Sanders Celebrity Golf Classic.

Red Skelton

Roy Rogers and his son.

With Jim McMahon, Houston Golf, 1987.

Lee Trevino and Johnny, 1986.

Telly Savalas

Jimmy Dean, Walt Garrison, and Johnny.

B. J. Thomas

Glen Campbell

Floyd Cramer

Mel Tillis

Johnny with Danny Cooksey, 1989.

Johnny and Minnie Pearl on MCN Award Show, 1982.

Eddie Rabbit, Kris Kristofferson, Johnny, and Moe Bandy, 1989.

10: The Musical Pits

After my contract was up with Warner Brothers, they didn't sign me again. I thought the whole world had fallen out from underneath me. I felt unwanted in the music business. I heard all my songs on the radio — "Lookin' For Love" . . . "Picking Up Strangers" . . . "Cherokee Fiddle" . . . "Hey, Bartender" . . . "You Can Bet Your Heart On Me" . . . "One in a Million" . . . "When You Fall in Love" . . . "Could Have Heard a Heart Break" . . . "Sounds Like Love To Me" — but I couldn't get arrested, much less a recording contract.

I didn't know where to go or who to turn to. I was running out of money and finally had to start playing for chicken feed in any little old bar. I'd start to walk in a bar to get a job and I'd be thinking back on my days at Gilley's and saying, "Oh God, please don't let me have to go back in the bars and sing every night with some house band like I used to have to do." My pride was bruised, and Gilley's was haunting me all over again. It was a hell of a fall from stardom.

As I began thinking of what to do I remembered that Irving Azoff, who had promised to make me a star with *Urban Cowboy* — and did — told me once that he wanted me on his label, at MCA Records. I wasted no time in calling him, and when I told him that Warner Brothers would not be signing me, he again told me he wanted me on his label. In fact, he said, "We had hits before, there's no reason we can't have hits again. Just consider yourself on MCA." He even went so far as to send people from MCA to Canada while I was up there doing a job, to meet me and take me around to some radio stations and introduce me as a new MCA recording artist. Well, lo and behold, that wasn't true. I was being bullshitted again.

Azoff would say, "I want you there, you're on the label . . . but talk to . . ." and then he'd name a few people. Now keep in mind, this guy is not small-time; he handled some big names. But when I talked with whomever he would tell me to talk with, they would say there was "no room on the label for you" or "you're not what we're looking for." I'd call Azoff back and he'd say, "Naw, I'll handle it."

We went back and forth like that for quite a while, and they all kept passing the buck. Finally, I found out what Azoff had said wasn't true. I wasn't going to be on MCA at all. Suddenly, Azoff didn't want to talk to me anymore.

So there I was — out in the cold. I couldn't get a record label. I didn't know what I was going to do, or where my future would go. I couldn't even figure out what had happened. It's a very helpless, frustrating feeling when you suddenly find yourself outside of it all, and it turns on you so fast that you don't even know what happened. All I could do was tread water.

I went through several years of nothing. The little money I had was evaporating by the day. I would take anything and sing anywhere to keep a few bucks coming in. Then I ran into Jack McFadden, Buck Owens's former manager. He found me after I got rid of Cryer and had spent just about all my money on lawyers who lost everything but the songs I wrote. Jack said he wanted to make my life easier, that he had always been a fan of mine. So, I signed a management contract with him.

It felt great just to be wanted. I thought, "Here we go . . . my career's back on the road again." This guy had handled Buck Owens, so surely things would start to happen. But it

ended up that Jack didn't do anything for me or my career.
Here I was, paying him fifteen percent to be my manager (not
to mention an additional ten percent to his booking agency)
and nothing was being done for my career. I was doing the
same few gigs I had been able to find on my own. No record-
ings, no commercials, no endorsements, no new songs, no
nothing. He did take some of the old stuff I had recorded at
Warner Brothers that never made it on an album and tried to
get some contracts with it. But he just couldn't do it. I told
him, "Jack, if that stuff was great then, Warner Brothers
would have kept me to begin with."

I finally had to tell him to forget it. I couldn't see paying
someone just so he could call himself my manager. He's a
great guy, believe me, but I didn't need a manager like that. It
was just an unnecessary expense.

Things were getting pretty thin about then. There were
times when Debbie and I didn't have any money. Fortunately,
my truck was paid for, and I was able to get a few concert
dates here and there through a guy named Reggie Mack who
worked at McFadden's booking agency.

Then, in 1988, Reggie introduced me to a fellow by the
name of Mick Lloyd. Mick and I cut a few songs that he financed. He liked what he heard and thought maybe some
fresh material would scare up a contract. So, Debbie and I
talked about it and decided that we had to scrape up some
money somehow and go for it. We knew it would truly be a roll
of the dice.

After getting together every dime we had, we financed
the remaining seven songs on the album. The album would
either bring us a record contract, or we'd be broke and I'd have
to work as a carpenter or something — anything to make a living. But we got some good songs, including a couple I wrote,
and Mick and I teamed up with a fellow named Mike Daniels
as co-producer. We went into the studio with the pickers and
made our attempt. The work took about a year.

I financed the thing myself. Paid everybody. Even
shopped it around to a couple of people, including Dick Whitehouse of Curb Records. I had met Dick at a concert we did in
Los Angeles to raise money to feed the hungry, the ranks of
which I thought I might soon be joining. I told him I was work-

ing on an album and asked if he would listen to it after we finished recording. He said he would and told me to bring it by.

After we finished, I immediately sent it to him, then Debbie and I just sat on pins and needles, waiting on the word. Before long he called and said, "Don't send it to anybody else." Then it got quiet as more time passed.

Finally, one morning in Montgomery, Alabama, Debbie and I were lying in bed at a Holiday Inn. I was working there for a few days, and Mick knew where to find me. We had just waked up and, as usual, I was wondering about the record deal when Mick called me and said, "Congratulations, we did it." I started hollering. I imagine the people staying in the rooms around ours probably thought Debbie was torturing me. But it was like a new start in life. I felt wanted again. It was such a relief for both Debbie and me, because she was beside me the whole time and she knew I had given my life to my profession.

When negotiations started for a recording contract, I told Mick, "I don't want anything . . . just them having me is good enough." I thought we were just going to have to give it to them. Mick handled the negotiations for me, though we had agreed early on that he would not be my manager per se. He was going to help me handle my career. I had decided that every time I had a manager, I had bad experiences.

Mick started talking with Curb and told me he would have something in a day or so — a Thursday, shortly thereafter, as a matter of fact. Well, that Thursday turned into Friday and I was getting anxious. Finally, on Friday he called and said, "I'll have something in a few hours."

A few hours passed while I had a couple of beers and paced. I called Mick. Still nothing, so I paced some more and had a couple more beers. I called Mick again, still nothing, then a couple more beers. By the end of the day I had had about twelve beers, then I found out that we weren't going to get an answer until Monday. I had to go through the weekend without knowing about the contract! I got so upset, with all that beer in me, I just puked.

Well, I almost went crazy until Monday came, but still nothing! Then Tuesday and Wednesday came with no word. It was getting ridiculous and I couldn't stand it. So, I just grabbed the phone and called Dick Whitehouse and said, "I've got to find out something about this contract . . . I'm going broke buying Maalox." That evening, I finally got the word: It was a done deal. I was on Curb Records.

As it turned out, they paid us back all the money Debbie and I had scraped together to finance the recording, and we signed a ten-album contract.

Return:
New Directions

As happens so often in this small-world business, co-producer Mick Lloyd and Johnny Lee crossed paths briefly, in 1977, as artists on GRT Records in Nashville. But they never really knew each other. It was through booking agent Reggie Mack that the two began working together in 1988. Lloyd says he was never really sure of what they could do together, though he always believed in Johnny's talent.

"The reason that I was interested in working with him in the beginning," Lloyd remembers, "was because of his great appeal in Japan. I had started doing a few things with that market, and it was clear to me that the Japanese were eager to buy Johnny's albums. The Japanese really like American music. They copy it all the time, and if they do the same with our music that they have with our cars and radios, before long they'll be selling American music — made in Japan, with Japanese artists — to fans in the United States. But they do really get into our music, and Johnny has quite a following there. So, when we went into the studio I figured, at worst, I would get something I could release in Japan. It was sort of like hedging my bets . . . if we didn't get the 'big prize' we were aiming for, we could at least have something I could put out in the Orient."

171

It was Johnny's ability to sing not just *Urban Cowboy*-style, honky-tonk songs, but a variety of country songs that sold Lloyd on the artist.

"I don't think anyone knew he could really sing," Lloyd speculates, "because they had placed him in that *Urban Cowboy* mold and everything he did sounded exactly the same. So, he never had to stretch out vocally, and most people didn't think he was that talented.

"But, they were wrong. I saw something that was totally different, and when we decided to go into the studio I told Johnny, 'Look, there's absolutely no point in doing "Lookin' For Love" because that's history . . . we've got to do something that's totally different and shows people what you can really do.' Up to that point, everything he did that was a hit . . . was basically from that *Urban Cowboy* formula. They just did one after another. In essence, what they did was they rode a horse until they killed it."

For a while after the *Urban Cowboy* fad had faded, Johnny's name was almost taboo in the country music industry. Lloyd even remembers the advice of others.

"People close to me," Lloyd says, "told me it was a losing situation and that I would not be successful because of things they had heard about Johnny's past. There were a lot of people who thought it would never work. I chose to ignore them."

Lloyd actually financed the production of the first few songs to get Lee a new sound that they could show to record companies. But Johnny and Debbie pooled their last remaining financial resources to take one last shot and pay for the recording of his album.

During a period of six months, songs, some of which Johnny wrote, were recorded, reworked, and recorded again to get the fresh sound that would ultimately provide Johnny's comeback album with the appropriate title *New Directions.* The hurdle that everyone then faced was getting someone to buy it. It was no small task. Just because an artist has an entire album on tape doesn't guarantee a label will pick it up. Record companies have thousands of auditions and complete albums on tape from would-be recording stars waiting for the big break. In Johnny's case, there would probably have been fewer doors slammed in his face had he not been an established recording artist who had lost his way in the business. His fault or not, the cliquish moguls of the recording industry had branded him a "has-been" with marital problems and drug and alcohol abuse, which spelled "liability" to the king makers of the industry. Most of the rumors perpetrated by the tabloids and people who wanted to make a buck off of Johnny's misfortune were being taken as fact by the leaders of the business. The result: no record deals, no way, for Johnny Lee.

It was a frustrating time for the singer. He knew he had talent, and he realized he had been treated unfairly. His best shot, as happens so often in the music business, was a friend of a friend who would ultimately come through with a deal. In this case, it was Dick Whitehouse of Curb Records. At first, however, Whitehouse was like all the others in the industry. He did not want to sign Lee to the label.

"I told Mick that I knew Johnny was looking for a label," Whitehouse recalls, "but I also told him at the very first, 'I am not interested in Johnny Lee . . . we will not be signing Johnny Lee to the label, so don't bother sending the tape.' And I said that based on my own predication of the music that he had produced over the period of time following 'Lookin' For Love,' as well as my own ideas as to the commercial potential of that music and my ability to work with the kind of music that I felt he had been cutting.

"That, coupled with the material that came across my desk from more than one source concerning him and his music, led me to believe there was nothing Johnny Lee would record that I would be interested in at all. I felt what he had been doing was making the same record over and over again, just changing the words. But Mick assured me that wasn't the case at all."

Despite his concerns, Whitehouse decided to afford Johnny the same opportunity he does any new talent that darkens his door with a tape. He let Johnny's music speak for itself. After all, he had promised Johnny and Lloyd at one of Johnny's concerts that he would at least give it a listen.

"It was Johnny's good music that swayed him," Lloyd says.

Whitehouse is more direct. "I was dead wrong! I couldn't believe it was Johnny Lee. He sounded great. It wasn't 'Lookin' For Love' for the ninety-eighth time. He looked better . . . had lost weight . . . just a delightful guy."

Whitehouse then remembered Johnny's concert. How an artist performs on stage is just as important to his potential for a record company as the sound he produces in studio.

"The audience loved him," Whitehouse recalls. "He handled himself magnificently on stage."

But while all of this was going on, Johnny was still just surviving. Like so many artists without a label or a hit, he was fading on the music scene, despite his strong presence on radio. Radio stations were keeping him in front of the audience because of their emphasis on golden oldies due to listener requests. As a rule, country music fans are the most loyal of fans; that, in addition to frequent radio play, gave Johnny pockets of popularity in places like California, Texas, and Canada. But it was still very difficult to make ends meet with only occasional shows in small towns rather than large city concert facilities. A few thousand dollars a show and a few shows a year did not go very far.

"It's a tough way to live," according to Lloyd. "You can survive, but it's not what you may have been used to before. It can be a big letdown in terms of dollars, prestige, and the quality of places you're playing."

But within days of Whitehouse hearing Johnny's new work, a deal was cut and Johnny was back on a label. With the first album, *New Directions,* finished, he began working on the second album of a ten-album contract with Curb. Now he and Curb are working to get him back on top of the charts. *New Directions* is the foundation of that effort. The image is different, as are the songs.

"People in the industry hear the new album," Lloyd says, "and they can't believe it's Johnny Lee, because it's not the Johnny Lee they heard sing the same kind of song over and over again during the *Urban Cowboy* days. It's very much like the change and comeback of Kenny Rogers after he left the First Edition in the late 1960s, went away, and returned with a new image and sound."

Johnny has never been afraid of hard work or doing whatever is necessary to get to the top. He is also a man who knows how important the fans and the people around him are. Johnny is always there to sign the last fan's autograph book or to do one more radio interview.

Says Lloyd, "You build loyalty with these people by being nice to them . . . they're your bread and butter . . . you lose them and you lose everything. He never antagonized the fans and he always had a good relationship with radio. Those guys have always liked him, and so they're more likely to give him a shot on a comeback effort than someone who was rude to them the first time around.

By country music standards, Johnny is still young. He has time to rebuild the career so many took turns stealing from him. Rather than suffer through the mismanagement he experienced for so many years, Johnny is taking an active role in directing his own career. Part of that "take control" attitude is the steady, straight building process that most artists have to go through, rather than the slingshot to the stars scenario he experienced with the release of the *Urban Cowboy* movie. He would like each song on each album to be of the high quality that lends itself to single release status, or that of a hit single. But he and Lloyd know that takes careful crafting and a lot of work on the stage and in the studio . . . beginning with *New Directions.*

"It's not the type of thing where we're looking for meteoric success with the first record out," Lloyd explains. "The whole idea is to build back-up solidly. At the same time, he's with a good booking agency, World Class Talent, which is doing the same thing — accelerating dates, putting him with other good acts, opening him with some of the majors, getting headlining spots himself, and spreading him into other areas where he never really ventured before."

Whitehouse and Curb Records are now glad they listened to the music rather than the rumors.

"It's working," Whitehouse says. "The initial acceptance is very pleasing to the record label."

Reward:
Paying Back the Fans

Celebrities carry with them a special power to influence people. It is that very power that makes a fan loyal to the star, whether a football star or a country singer. Former Dallas Cowboy tight end Preston Pearson says, "You have to give back something to the fans for all the support they give you to begin with . . . and you have to remember, you influence people, be it a youngster who looks up to his favorite football hero or an adult who follows a favorite entertainer."

Johnny Lee learned that lesson early in his career, as have most country singers. Their fans expect them to be a friend . . . and a friend is always happy to see you and spend at least a few moments with you. Most country music artists know to at least act like they want to mingle with the fans, because country music fans stick with their favorite entertainers year after year, through celebrated hardships and glory, and career pinnacles. During an interview on the radio music program "Country Crossroads," Dick Clark, who has been at the heart of the industry for more than three decades, said, "Country music fans are the most loyal in the world . . . I can show you rock and roll entertainers who were 'has-beens' six months after they made it to the top."

Johnny and Debbie know exactly what the fans mean to them and they show their appreciation every chance they get. After a show, Johnny will spend hours signing autographs and talking — not chatting, but really talking — with the fans who are, in turn, genuinely touched by the singer's down-to-earth manner. Debbie likewise fields questions and many times will smile, take someone's hand, and say, "He'll be happy to talk with you just as soon as he's talked with this nice lady." Then she'll converse with the person like a gracious party hostess attending to the wants of her guests.

Their attitude of giving themselves to the public extends far beyond the autographs and conversations with fans backstage. The Lees are very involved in charity fund-raising work, ranging from causes like POWs and MIAs to helping the mentally retarded and feeding and housing the homeless. Most of Johnny's efforts are made in celebrity golf tournaments, auctions, and music shows to raise money. He's a regular when it comes to helping out the Home of Guiding Hands and even hosts a pro-am golf tournament that bears his name: the Johnny Lee Pro-Am Golf Tournament for the Home of Guiding Hands. The tournament raises about $20,000 a year for the mentally retarded residents of the home, located about twenty-five miles east of San Diego. Like so many of the charities Johnny helps, he takes a personal interest in the tournament and its associated activities.

One of the founders of the home, Joe Famme, says, "I approached Johnny about the golf tournament several years ago, while he was still singing with Gilley. He seemed very excited about working with the home and building up the tournament. It has grown every year, as have the donations." The home gets much of its funding through the State of California's Medical Program, but still relies on events like the annual golf tournament, held each September, to meet its budget. The tournament has become the single largest fund-raiser of all of the home's fund-raising activities each year.

Set at the Singing Hills Country Club near San Diego, the pro-am attracts a great number of pros and scores of amateurs anxious to make a donation and play with a pro or celebrity player like Johnny. It began as a day of golf and a night of entertainment. Now there are several days of golf, with evening events that are capped off with a big barbecue at the end of the week. Johnny performs and many times invites some of the children of the home up on stage to sing and dance with him. Famme says it's hard to tell who is having the most fun: "These kids are like his own . . . he loves them."

KSON Radio promotions director Steve Sapp agrees. Having known Johnny for several years, he has seen how he gets involved.

"My impressions of Johnny are superior. He and Debbie are really dedicated to the home's cause. It began the first year he came out to help with the fund-raising tournament for the home. He got here a couple of days early that year, and was supposed to take a tour of the home, meet some of the people, then leave. It was scheduled to last about forty minutes. He got so wrapped up with those kids he wouldn't leave. He started joking and playing with them. They started having a great time with him, pulling his cowboy hat off and arm wrestling. In fact, every year now he has to have the traditional arm wrestling match with one of the residents of the home . . .

"During the show the first year, Johnny stopped between songs to talk about the home and suddenly asked if he and Debbie could come back the following year and help again, which naturally brought a standing ovation. Now he shows up for a week prior to the tournament every year, taking time from a touring schedule which, everyone knows, means money out of his pocket, and he and Debbie play host for the events that have now stretched to the better part of a week . . . I don't think you could pull Johnny away from the fund-raiser if you tried. You see so many of these charities and benefits and tournaments in which an actor or an athlete or some sort of celebrity puts his or her name on the event but they just really don't get behind it. In Johnny's case . . . he's into the things he works for and the people who benefit from them. Each year, when he does the big show at the end of the week of fund-raising for the Home of Guiding Hands, I watch him as he brings some of the kids up to the stage to let them sing and have a good time with him, and the love there is so real."

Whatever inconvenience may result from such devotion to a cause, Johnny and Debbie look at it as the right thing to do to directly help a public that has seen them through thick and thin.

11:   Philosophy According to Lee

I once compared the music business to owning a boat. A man has worked to save up his money and buy the boat of his dreams — a big, beautiful, shiny new boat. But lo and behold he's got to find a marina to dock the big boat and pay so much every month to keep it there. And before he knows it, there are barnacles attached all over the bottom of the boat and he's spending a lot of his time scraping them off. It's the same way in the music business. Once you get something going, you've got all these barnacles attaching themselves to you that you have to keep scraping off. And I've had my share of barnacles.

But I'll never quit the business I'm in. It's my life. Some people I know were satisfied to work their entire lives in one of the refineries at home. And I really feel that many of them enjoyed it. It was probably, in some ways, as rewarding to them as some of the rewards I've known in my profession. I think doing a job you're proud of, whether a good show on stage or a good shift at the plant, gives you the same feeling of satisfaction.

My uncle is about to retire from a refinery in Texas City where he's worked all his life. It was a job that he was good at.

179

In fact, they're trying to talk him into not retiring. But he's got such a good retirement plan set up that he's going to live comfortably for the rest of his life. He's happy.

Between record deals I look at myself and wonder how I am going to take care of my wife and family when I am his age. What am I going to have then? Will people still want to come and see me play when I'm sixty years old? Sometimes it scares me, then it pisses me off because I think about how I've been screwed around by vultures. They are the people who make it hard for you to be secure for the rest of your life. And they are out there by the hundreds, under every rock you kick out of the way.

Just from *Urban Cowboy* and the songs I've written alone, I should be independently wealthy, with money set aside for retirement and no worries about my old age. I'll guarantee you my uncle and folks like him will get the retirement money that refinery set aside for them.

Without a doubt, I've learned several valuable lessons about life. But I think everyone does; it's part of aging. Like most people, I wish I had known then what I know now, because if I had, I'd have been one slick son of a bitch. As it stands, I would be afraid to figure how much I got screwed out of, just because of my own sheer ignorance. But aside from the fact that I finally learned not to trust my financial situation to anyone but myself, I've learned to put things in perspective.

Family, for instance, is a priority in my life. I know I'm lucky to have the things I have and to have done some of the things I did, but my wife, my little girl, my mother, aunts, and uncles are more important to me than anything. I've always tried to stay close to my family, but needless to say, the lifestyle didn't always allow it — sometimes to the point of causing some real problems for me. When my Uncle Gene died, I was on the road with Mickey. Cryer made me believe that I couldn't miss those concerts, at any cost. I missed my uncle's funeral . . . and I hated myself after that. But I felt then that I was under an iron thumb, and I simply didn't know any better.

I know that my lifestyle is a gamble, a poker game in

which I've sometimes drawn a bad hand — or someone across the table has pulled an ace from his sleeve. But as a graduate from the old school of hard knocks, top five in the class I might add, I also know that this gambler's counting the cards on the table nowadays. And it's going to take a smart son of a bitch to get me now.

Memorial:
A Place Called Gilley's

By the time *Urban Cowboy* was filmed during the summer of 1979, Gilley's was the world's largest honky-tonk, and the man with his name in neon lights above the door had a string of hits that stretched across Pasadena and Houston and eventually the nation. Mickey Gilley's piano-playing hands were covered in gold and diamond rings. He owned two pickup trucks, a fancy car, half of a recording studio, and a share of the financial interest in the night club.

But along with the fame and money came the problems. Court appearances ranged from patent questions concerning the rights of the mechanical bulls marketed after they were made successful by the movie *Urban Cowboy,* to lawsuits from people injured while riding the bulls, to paternity suits from anyone wanting a little publicity and money from the Gilley name. There were problems with businesses near the club, upset at large outdoor events like the Fourth of July party in 1981. Many claimed the crowds, estimated at about 10,000, would pour into the area, disrupting business and even the daily operation of a nearby hospital. Some feared a lack of police personnel in Pasadena might cause the police force to buckle under the pressure of maintaining law and order and result in serious problems.

182

The most serious problems, however, were internal. Johnny and Mickey both claimed Sherwood Cryer cheated them out of money. Before it was all said and done, there were harsh words — even violence.

Finally, the image, the glitz, and the neon lights that were Gilley's faded after nearly two decades of success when Cryer declared the club closed in 1989. Cryer had just lost $17 million to Gilley in a lawsuit during the summer of 1988. Mickey Gilley and Johnny Lee had long been in disputes with Cryer over money owed and property owned. In March of 1989, a break-in and theft of equipment at the club's recording studio was the last straw. Cryer declared bankruptcy, and a judge ordered the club closed indefinitely. Cryer told reporters in Houston that it was over.

The *Urban Cowboy* era, long since faded across most of the rest of the country like an old pair of blue jeans, had finally seen the setting sun over its birthplace in Pasadena, Texas.